THE CAPITOL
INSIDE & OUT

DEDICATION

*To my wife, Jean, who puts up with a history
nerd for a husband.*

*To my boss, mentor and friend,
Jim Oberstar, who gave me my first guided
tour of the Capitol.*

*To my sister, Joan,
whom I promised to mention somewhere
in this book. Hi, Joni!*

And to Mom (1909-2002)

THE CAPITOL INSIDE & OUT

Stories of the People and Events
that Give Life to Washington's
Most Historic Building.

By Jim Berard

Introduction by Senator Eugene J. McCarthy

EPM Publications, Inc.

Marshall, Virginia

Library of Congress Cataloging-in-Publication Data

Berard, Jim, 1952-
    The Capitol inside & out : stories of the people and events that give life to Washington's
most historic building / by Jim Berard ; introduction by Eugene J. McCarthy.
        p. cm.
    Includes bibliographical references.
    ISBN 1-889324-24-8
    1. United States Capitol (Washington, D.C.)–Anecdotes. 2. United States–Politics and
government--Anecdotes. 3. Washington (D.C.)–Buildings, structures, etc.--Anecdotes. I.
Title: Capitol inside and out. II. Title.

F204.W5B47 2003
975.3`02--dc21

                                                                                            2003049193

Cover and Book Design: Tom Huestis
Cover Illustration: R.J. Matson

Cover Illustration:

FRONT ROW:
Jim Wright, Daniel Webster, Everett Dirksen, Henry Clay, Abraham Lincoln,
John Calhoun, John Glenn, Millicent Fenwick, Davy Crockett

MIDDLE ROW:
Bella Abzug, Mark Twain, Will Rogers, Sam Rayburn, Paul Simon,
George Washington, Joseph Cannon, Tip O'Neill

BACK ROW:
James Garfield, Sam Houston, John Quincy Adams, Thomas U. Walter,
Constantino Brumidi

Contents

The story of the Capitol is intricately entwined with the story of the institution it houses, the United States Congress. So, for a complete understanding of the building and its functions, it's helpful to have a basic understanding of how Congress works.

The Legislative Branch

Congress is one of three branches of the federal government created by the Constitution. It is known as the *legislative* branch and consists of the Senate and the House of Representatives. The other two branches are the *executive* branch, headed by the President, and the *judicial* branch, which consists of the Supreme Court and the lower federal courts.

It is the job of Congress to create laws. The President and the executive branch are charged with implementing the laws, and the courts interpret the laws when differences arise. The three branches are equal in stature and power, and exercise a system of checks and balances over each other. For example, the President may keep a law from taking effect, or the Supreme Court may determine that the law runs contrary to the Constitution and overturn it. Congress, at the same time, must approve Presidential appointments, including the appointment of justices to the Supreme Court, and has control over spending, including the salaries paid to the President and the justices.

Another check Congress holds on the executive and judicial branches is the power of impeachment and removal from office. When a federal official or federal judge is accused of wrongdoing, the House can investigate and bring articles of impeachment against that person. If the House votes to impeach, the matter is sent over to the Senate for resolution. The Senate hears testimony and evidence and can vote to remove the person from office. In its history, the House has impeached two Presidents, Andrew Johnson in 1868 and Bill Clinton in 1999. In both cases, the Senate failed to reach the two-thirds majority voted needed to remove the person from office.

Both the House and Senate have the power to remove their own Members for misconduct. Each chamber has its own rules for such proceedings. Neither the President nor the Supreme Court can remove a Member of Congress from office.

The Great Compromise

The delegates to the Constitutional Convention in Philadelphia in 1787 had a problem: how to make sure all states are fairly represented in the new government they were creating for the United States.

The government was going to have a legislature. That was a given. A legislature—a governing body made up of representatives of the citizenry—is a necessary part of any democratic government. What hung up the Founding Fathers was how to apportion those representatives to each of the 13 states.

The larger states said the answer was obvious: apportion the legislators according to population. The larger states would get more, but they also have more citizens, so it would be fair.

The smaller states thought otherwise. They reminded their large-state colleagues that the country was a union of sovereign states, and they felt all states should have an equal say in the affairs of the new government.

Finally, after much debate, the delegates reached a compromise. The legislature would consist of two houses: the Senate, where each state has equal representation, and the House of Representatives, where representation is apportioned by population. The Congress of the United States was born.

The Senate

Each state elects two Senators. Since there are currently 50 states, that means there are currently 100 Senators. Senators serve six-year terms, which are staggered so one-third of the Senate seats are up for election every two years.

For many years, Senators were elected by the legislatures of their home states. In 1913, the 17th Amendment to the Constitution called for all Senators to be elected directly by the people. Governors may still make appointments to the Senate to fill a vacancy when a Senator dies, retires or otherwise leaves office before the end of his or her term. Such appointments are usually temporary until an election can be held. Laws governing this process vary from state to state.

The Senate shares responsibility for making laws with the House. The Senate has the additional duties of confirming Presidential appointments and ratifying international treaties.

Under the Constitution, the Vice President of the United States is the presiding officer of the Senate, but only votes to break a tie. In modern practice, the Vice President only shows up in the Senate when a tie vote is expected.

The rest of the time the presiding officer is either the President *Pro-Tempore* or a designee. The President Pro Tempore (or *Pro Tem*) is traditionally the senior member of the majority party in the Senate. A junior member of the majority party is usually designated to preside over most routine sessions of the Senate.

Day-to-day business in the Senate is controlled by the Majority Leader.

The Senate generally functions under rules that allow unlimited debate. This has given rise to the practice of the Senate *filibuster*, a long speech designed to stop action on a particular piece of business. Filibusters by one or a combination of Senators have been known to last for days. Filibustering Senators would recite poetry or read recipes to hold the floor. Sen. Strom Thurmond of South Carolina holds the record for the longest speech in Senate history: 24 hours, 18 min.

Over the years, rules have been adopted to limit, but not eliminate, the filibuster. In 1917, the Senate adopted a rule that allowed a two-thirds majority vote to end debate. This is called the *cloture* rule. In 1975, the threshold was reduced to a three-fifths majority (60 votes in the current Senate) to invoke cloture. Modern rules also allow the Senate to move on to other business without ending the filibuster. This two-track approach allows the filibustering Senator to retain the floor if the Senate should return to the issue. In effect, action on that issue is stalled without tying up the rest of the business before the Senate.

The House of Representatives

The other legislative body created by the Constitution is the House of Representatives. Members of the House are elected for two-year terms. The entire membership is up for election every two years.

Representatives are apportioned to the states according to population. There are 435 seats in the House. This number has been fixed since 1913. Each state gets at least one Representative and the rest of the seats are divided up according to the latest census. California, the most populous state, currently has 53 seats in the House.

States with more than one Representative are divided into Congressional Districts. Each district then elects one Representative. In the past, the states had a great deal of freedom in determining the size and shape of their Congressional Districts. The courts have since determined that the districts must be of equal population, or as close to equal as possible. The courts based this decision on the need to give everyone in the state an equal vote.

Unlike Senators, Representatives cannot be appointed to their office, even to fill a vacancy. They must be elected. (There have been two recent exceptions to this rule. More on that later.)

The Constitution requires that all tax and spending bills begin in the House. In a Presidential election, the House of Representatives is called upon to break the deadlock if no candidate receives a majority of electoral votes.

The presiding officer of the House of Representatives is the Speaker of the House. The Speaker is elected by the entire membership of the House at the beginning of each Congress. (In modern practice, votes in the election for Speaker fall along party lines, so the successful candidate is always from the majority party in the House.)

The Speaker is second in line for the Presidency, after the Vice President.

Because of its size, the House has rules that place strict limits on debate. Representatives do not have the freedom to filibuster that Senators have. Very often, Members are only recognized for one minute or even 30 seconds to speak on an issue before the House.

The House allows two opportunities during the legislative day for Members to speak on any issue they choose. At the beginning of the day, a limited number of Members are recognized on a first-come, first-served basis to speak for one minute on any topic. Such speeches could comment on the news of the day, preview the debate on an issue before the House later that day, or congratulate a local championship sports team.

At the end of the day, Members are allowed to speak for as much as an hour or more under Special Orders. These speeches take place after the House has completed its legislative business for the day. On occasion, groups of Representatives will present Special Orders speeches all night long to direct attention to a given issue. The House Chamber is usually empty during Special Orders,

but these speeches allow Members to make their views part of the official record of the day's business. The speeches are also televised, reaching a national cable audience.

The Legislative Process: Laws and Sausages

The great German statesman Otto Von Bismarck is said to have said, "Laws are like sausages. It is better not to see them being made."

Like stuffing sausages, making our nation's laws can be a messy process. Watching it could be hard on the appetite.

The legislative process can also be inefficient and frustrating, even maddening. Legislators are often forced to make difficult compromises. As Rep. James L. Oberstar of Minnesota once described the process, "Sometimes you just have to hold your nose and vote."

Despite its unappetizing nature, this inefficient process for making our laws has served America well for more than two centuries. Indeed, it is designed to be difficult in order to ensure that only the most deserving bills survive and to avoid frequent and capricious changes to our nation's laws.

Every federal law begins life as a bill introduced in either the House or the Senate. Any member can introduce a bill on any subject. The sponsor of a bill can also ask other members of the chamber to sign on to the bill as cosponsors. Attracting many cosponsors is a good way to show how much support the bill has and how likely it is to pass when brought up for a vote.

Once a bill is introduced, it is assigned to a committee of jurisdiction. For example, a bill on farm issues would be referred to the Agriculture Committee. The committee then studies the bill, often assigning it to a subcommittee. The subcommittee may hold hearings on the bill to collect testimony from experts on the issue, industry representatives or government officials. The subcommittee may also make amendments to the bill. Finally it will decide if the bill should be approved for review by the full committee. This is done in what is called a *mark-up* session.

The full committee then takes the subcommittee's report and holds its own mark-up session, where the entire committee membership can debate and amend the bill, and vote to report it to the full House or Senate, depending on where the bill originated.

When the bill is brought up before the full chamber, it faces another round of debate and possible amendments. If the bill is approved, it is then sent over to the other chamber, where the process begins all over again. If the House and Senate pass different versions of the bill, the two chambers appoint members to a *conference committee* to work out the differences and craft a compromise bill. Once a bill is approved in the exact same form in both the House and Senate, it is sent to the President.

If the President signs the bill, it becomes law. If the President disapproves of the bill, he can kill it. This is called the Presidential *veto* (Latin for "I forbid."). Congress can override the President's veto with a two-thirds vote in each chamber. If supporters of the bill cannot muster a two-thirds vote in one of the two chambers, the measure is dead.

This is the basic procedure for moving a bill through the legislative process. There are also expedited procedures that can be used when time is critical or the bill is routine in nature. These shortcuts in the process are usually used with the agreement of the leadership of both parties in the chamber, often in conjunction with the leadership of the other chamber, and the President.

Persons serving in either the House or Senate are Members of Congress. Members of the Senate are generally addressed as "Senator." Members of the House are called "Representative," or, more commonly, "Congressman" (or "Congresswoman").

Lame Ducks and Appointees

As you read this book, you will notice that most years of service begin in odd-numbered years.

Regular elections for Senators and Representatives are held in November of even-numbered years, but those elected in November don't take office until Congress reconvenes the following January. Likewise, Members of Congress who are retiring or who lose the election in November retain their seats until the new Members are sworn in, again in January.

There are some exceptions to this rule. In the early days of the Senate, Senators were elected by their state legislatures. These elections could take place any time during the year.

Also in the Senate, it is not unusual for an outgoing Senator to resign in the two months between the election and the assembly of the new Congress in order to allow the newly elected successor to take the seat and get a head start in seniority. When Congress holds a special session during this interim period, it is called a *lame duck* session, because many of the Members attending will be at the end of their Congressional service. In two unusual moves, the House seated two newly elected Members for a lame duck session instead of making them wait until the new Congress convened. Rep. Steve Largent of Oklahoma was seated for a lame duck session of the 103rd Congress in November, 1994. Largent was appointed by the Governor of his state following the resignation of his predecessor, James Inhofe. (Inhofe had just won election to the Senate.). The Governor claimed state law gave him the authority to make the appointment. Although Largent's early seating was unprecedented, the matter was referred to a committee, which took no action. Once the short lame-duck session adjourned, the matter became moot.

Similarly, the House tacitly accepted the appointment of Representative-elect Jim Ryun of Kansas in 1996. Ryun had just won election to the seat vacated by Rep. Sam Brownback, who had won election to the Senate. Like Largent, Ryun was appointed by the Governor to fill the seat in a lame-duck session, and the House did not refuse the appointment.

Party Animals

In the course of this book, you will see references to several political parties, some of which may be unfamiliar to you. Not surprising. A lot of Members of Congress have worn many different party labels over the 200-plus years of the nation's history.

Political parties, as we now know them, didn't exist when the nation was established after the Revolution. Still, the Founders did find themselves breaking into factions. George Washington, John Adams and others who supported the adoption of the Constitution, with a strong, unifying central government, became known as Federalists. Thomas Jefferson and others who favored keeping most of the governmental power in the hands of the states, were at first called Anti-Federalists, then adopted the name Democratic-Republicans. This name was often shortened to either Democrats or Republicans, which can be really confusing when viewed in the light of our present two-party system.

Jefferson's Democratic-Republican party developed into the modern Democratic party with the election of Andrew Jackson in 1828. By then, the Federalist party had faded and a new anti-Jacksonian party, the Whigs, emerged. The Whig party took its name from a 17th Century faction in England that favored limitations on the power of the king.

Another party with some modest success in the early to mid-1800's was the American party, often called the "Know Nothings." The party got its unflattering nickname because of its secrecy. When questioned about the party's activities, a member would simply say he "knows nothing." The Know Nothings opposed immigration, and were strongly anti-Catholic.

The modern Republican party emerged in the 1850's, and attracted a combination of Whigs, Know Nothings and Northern Democrats opposed to slavery. Its first successful Presidential candidate was Abraham Lincoln in 1860.

Since the end of the Civil War in 1865, the two major parties we have today, Democratic and Republican, have dominated national politics.

Sometimes Members of Congress change their party membership. John Quincy Adams served in the Senate as a Federalist, was elected President as a Democrat-Republican, and was subsequently elected to the House as a Whig. Over the years, other Members of Congress have been elected as independents, or have left their party to become independents. Sen. Wayne Morse of Oregon was elected to the Senate as a Republican in 1944, left the party to become an independent, and finished his Senate career in 1972 as a Democrat.

IN COMMITTEE

The House Transportation and Infrastructure Committee meets for a mark-up session in °the Rayburn House Office Building.

PHOTO CREDIT:
Jim Berard

1

A Capitol
for the Capital

Washington, D.C. in 1791 was very different from the capital city of today. The new home for the federal government was mostly forests, farms and wetlands. A French engineer named Pierre Charles L'Enfant was hired to design the new city and carve a world-class capital out of the wilderness. L'Enfant selected a site called Jenkins' Hill, a stately plateau 88 feet above the Potomac River, as the site for the new home of Congress, the Capitol. L'Enfant called Jenkins' Hill, "a pedestal waiting for a monument."

A Monument for Jenkins' Hill

In 1793, Dr. William Thornton, a British physician living in the West Indies, won a design competition for the new Capitol. He was awarded $500 and a building lot in the city. Thornton designed a building with a central section topped with a low dome, flanked by two wings housing the legislative chambers. President George Washington's administration later adopted an interior floorplan by architect Stephan Hallett and decided to give him equal credit with Thornton for the design of the Capitol.

Construction on the Capitol began later that year. James Hoban, who designed the White House, became the supervising architect in charge of the project's first phase. Hallett, working under Hoban, directly supervised the work. President Washington laid the cornerstone on September 18, 1793, in a Masonic ceremony.

Washington, himself a Freemason, wore a ceremonial apron. He used a silver trowel to spread mortar on the stone and a marble gavel to symbolically tap it into place. The stone was set atop an engraved silver plate and Washington placed corn and poured oil and wine on the stone.

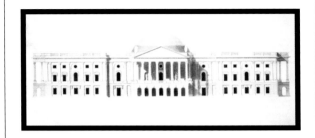

GOOD THING THEY DIDN'T SING

Newspapers of the day reported that the cornerstone ceremony concluded with "awful prayer" and an artillery salute. The dignitaries then celebrated by feasting on barbecued ox.

("Awful" can also mean "full of awe," or "reverential," as well as its modern meaning of something bad or to be avoided. Still, use of the term "awful prayer" today seems to be an unusual choice of words.)

The north wing of the building was the first to be completed and, in 1800, Congress, the Supreme Court, and the Library of Congress moved in. In 1801, a low, oval building was constructed for the House of Representatives. The temporary structure was so uncomfortable, the Congressmen nicknamed it "The Oven."

Architect Benjamin Henry Latrobe took over the project in 1803. Under his supervision, the south (House) wing of the building was opened for business in 1807 and completed in 1811.

Enter the British

In 1812, only 31 years after the end of the American Revolution, the United States went to war with Great Britain for a second time. In August of 1814, British troops landed at Benedict, Maryland, and marched on the young nation's capital.

The British attackers ransacked and set fire to the government buildings in the city, including the still unfinished Capitol. They spread gunpowder paste on furniture from the Congressional chambers and used books from the Library of Congress to fuel the flames. When the British troops withdrew, the Capitol was, as Latrobe called it, "a magnificent ruin."

Latrobe worked to restore the two burned-out wings of the Capitol for nearly three years. Charles Bulfinch took over the project in 1818, and had the building ready for reoccupancy the next year. In the interim, Congress met in the Old Brick Capitol.

* * *

THE OLD BRICK CAPITOL

After Adm. Cockburn's British sacked and burned the unfinished Capitol, Congress needed a new place to meet. There was even some sentiment to move the government out of Washington and establish a new capital further inland, where it would be less vulnerable to foreign invaders.

Congress decided the government should stay put, however, and had a brick structure built at the corner of First St. and Maryland Ave. NE to act as a temporary home. Congress met in the Old Brick Capitol from 1815 to 1819.

President James Monroe took his oath of office there in 1817. Monroe's inaugural set the precedent of holding the ceremony outside because the House and Senate could not agree on which chamber to use. The outdoor ceremony also allowed for a larger crowd of spectators, making it more democratic.

When Congress returned to the Capitol, the brick building was converted into a rooming house.

In Civil War times, the building was converted to a prison. Confederate spy Belle Boyd

was a guest there. So was Mary Surratt, the only woman hanged in the plot to assassinate President Lincoln.

The Old Capitol Prison, as it was later known, was demolished after the war.

The Supreme Court now occupies the site.

* * *

The Too-Tall Dome

Once the House and Senate wings were restored and reoccupied, Bulfinch turned his attention to the final phase of the building's construction, the center section and dome. As the architect prepared his designs, pressure mounted to build a dome higher than the one included in Thornton's original plan, even higher than Bulfinch himself would have preferred.

Bulfinch sketched several designs for the dome and submitted them to President James Monroe and his Cabinet, showing domes of different heights. He included one drawing of a dome he thought was too tall, in order to provide a comparison and make his preferred design look better.

To Bulfinch's surprise, the President and his advisors chose the tallest design for the Capitol dome.

Once completed, the dome rose 140 feet above the ground and 70 feet above the roof of the Capitol; the inner dome was 96 feet above the Rotunda floor. At the top of the dome, a round skylight, or *oculus*, 24 feet in diameter, brought light into the Rotunda.

The dome included a staircase to an observation deck from which visitors could enjoy an unparalleled view of the city. One visitor lost her footing and fell through the skylight. She managed to catch hold of a sash bar and saved herself from a likely fatal fall to the stone floor of the Rotunda.

OLD BRICK

The Old Brick Capitol was built as a temporary home for Congress while the Capitol was being rebuilt after the 1814 fire. The building later served as a boarding house and a prison. The Supreme Court building now stands on the site.

A Bigger House for a Growing Country

As the nation grew, so did Congress. By 1850, the country had grown to 31 states, and the House and Senate chambers were too small to accommodate the new legislators. Plans were drawn up to expand the Capitol.

Philadelphia architect Thomas U. Walter was awarded the job of adding new House and Senate wings to the Capitol. The House of Representatives moved into its new chamber in 1857; Senators occupied their new home in 1859.

With Walter's additions, the Capitol was now twice as wide as it was under the original Thornton design. Bulfinch's dome was too small for the larger building, and in 1855 Congress voted to replace the wooden dome with a larger one made from cast-iron. The new additions gave the Capitol the appearance we recognize today.

A Symbol of National Survival

When the Civil War broke out in 1861, the Capitol served as a military barracks, hospital and bakery. The Capitol became a symbol to the nation that the Union would survive. At the end of the war in 1865, an assassin's bullet took the life of President Lincoln, and his body was brought to lie in state in the Capitol. Work on the expanded Capitol continued through the war and was completed in 1868.

A RARE VIEW

One of the oldest known photographs of the Capitol, this daguerreotype from 1846 shows the building with Bulfinch's dome of wood and copper instead of the cast iron dome that is so recognizable today. Also missing are the new House and Senate wings that were added in the 1850's.

PHOTO CREDIT:
Library of Congress.
Neg. no. LC-USZC4-46801

GOING UP

Construction on the Capitol's new dome continued despite the outbreak of the Civil War in 1861.

PHOTO CREDIT:
Library of Congress.
Neg. no. LC-USZC4-4583

19

Over the years, many improvements were made to the Capitol. Bulfinch added the first terraces along the West Front in 1826. Running water was added in 1832. Gas lights were installed in the 1840's. The Capitol received its first elevator in 1874. From 1884 to 1891, workers expanded the marble terraces on the West Front of the building, and a gas explosion in 1898 prompted further improvements to protect the Capitol from fire.

★ ★ ★

SLAVE LABOR

In one of history's great ironies, the Capitol of the United States of America, the land of the free, the beacon of liberty in the world, was built, in part, by slaves.

The original construction of the Capitol and the addition of the new House and Senate wings and the cast-iron dome took place when slavery was legal in Washington, D.C. Slave laborers were lent out by their masters to work on these projects. They worked alongside European immigrants attracted to Washington by the promise of work. The immigrants were paid a daily wage for their labor. The slaves were not. Instead, their owners were paid for the slaves' services.

Most of the records list only first names of the slaves who worked on the building, so little is known about them. One named Philip Reid, though, is an exception.

Reid was the slave of Clark Mills, the foundryman who cast the bronze Statue of Freedom that stands atop the Capitol dome. When Mills' superintendent quit in a dispute over wages, Reid took over the job. Reid became a free man a few years later when slavery was abolished.

In 2000, Reps. J.C. Watts of Oklahoma and John L. Lewis of Georgia introduced legislation to create a commission to recommend a proper memorial for the Capitol grounds to recognize the contribution Reid and the other slaves made to the construction of the Capitol.

On the floor of the House, Lewis said slavery is part of the history of our country. We may not be proud of it, but we should not run away from it, he said.

"These men, these slaves, laid the very foundation of our democracy," Lewis told the House.

Watts and Lewis enlisted Republican Spencer Abraham of Michigan and Democrat Blanche Lambert Lincoln of Arkansas to introduce a companion bill in the Senate. Because of its sponsors, the bill was appropriately dubbed the "Abraham-Lincoln" bill.

The resolution was adopted in October, 2000.

★ ★ ★

Hot Times

When the Capitol was built, there was no such thing as air conditioning. Congress seldom met in warm-weather months, so little thought was given to the need to cool the legislative chambers during the hot, muggy Washington summers.

When the new House and Senate chambers were built in the late 1850's, architect Walter and Superintendent Meigs designed them without windows, instead using steam-powered fans for ventilation.

Just a few years after the House and Senate moved into their spacious new quarters, the Civil War broke out. The conduct of the war required Congress to stay in session year round to enact emergency legislation. The House and Senate chambers became so stuffy during the summer of 1862 that the Senate considered having its wing rebuilt to move the chamber closer to the outer wall to allow windows to bring fresh air into the room.

The Senate never acted on those plans and Congress had to suffer for another 66 years until the House and Senate chambers were air conditioned in 1928-29.

WHERE DID CONGRESS, ER, GO?

The Capitol was built in the days before indoor plumbing, making necessary the installation of facilities known as, well, necessaries.

Also called privies, necessaries were rooms or small buildings that served as toilets before running water and indoor plumbing made the modern bathroom possible.

In the Capitol's earliest days, architects Hoban and Latrobe dealt with the issue of privies. In 1800, the first wooden privy was installed just a month before Congress moved in. The structure was 70 feet long and 13 feet high. In 1803, Latrobe complained that the original design for the Capitol's interior, especially the House wing, had many defects, including no "closets of convenience." Latrobe's redesign of the wing provided for privies on the first floor. These indoor privies likely employed canvas bags to catch waste. The bags had to be regularly changed and emptied by attendants.

In 1826, architect Bulfinch moved the privies outdoors to courtyards created by the new terraces along the West Front. By 1834, the systems incorporated gutters and downspouts to flush basins with rain water from cisterns on the building's roof. The valves to flush the privies were activated when the door opened and closed.

The addition of the new House and Senate extensions in the 1850's allowed the first modern flush toilets to be installed in the Capitol. The new water closets used iron pipes to carry waste down to a main sewer line.

In 1900, one hundred years after Congress moved into its home, modern plumbing was installed in the oldest sections of the Capitol.

And necessaries were no longer necessary.

East Front Extension

The last major change to the Capitol in its first 200 years was the extension of the East Front, begun in 1958 and completed in 1962. Exact copies of the sandstone facade of the original building were made in marble, preserving the Capitol's appearance. The old exterior walls were left in place and can be seen along some corridors in the East Front extension.

The project extended the east facade of the structure by 32.5 feet, adding office and meeting space, providing the structure with greater stability and giving the building a more durable exterior.

LONELY COLUMNS

When the East Front of the Capitol was copied in marble for the new extensions in 1958-62, the old sandstone columns from the center portico were removed and placed in storage for possible future use. Each column stands 30 feet tall, measures 36 inches across at the base, and weighs 20 tons. The pillars were carved from stone quarried at Aquia Creek Quarry in Virginia and floated up the Potomac River on barges. They had stood at the main entrance to the Capitol for more than 130 years.

STANDING ALONE

The original sandstone columns from the center portico of the Capitol's East Front now stand alone and lonely at the National Arboretum in Washington.

PHOTO CREDIT:
Jim Berard

In 1984, 22 of the original 24 columns were moved to the National Arboretum in Northeast Washington. (One of the columns was deemed too damaged to use again; another was held back for other uses.)

In 1988, the 22 columns were erected around a rectangular courtyard at the Arboretum. The courtyard was paved with stone from the old East Front steps. The columns were meant to give the illusion of an ancient Greek temple, although some observers would liken it more to a modern interpretation of an ancient Greek ruin.

★ ★ ★

Lost and Found

Considering all the pomp and ceremony with which President Washington laid the Capitol's cornerstone, one would think better care would have been taken to remember where he put it.

In 1993, the Architect of the Capitol set out to find the building's cornerstone for the 200th anniversary of the ceremony. The only news account of the day indicated that the stone was laid in the building's southeast corner. But which southeast corner?

Traditionally, it was assumed that the ceremony took place at the southeast corner of the first section to be built, the north (Senate) wing. A plaque on the wall near the Old Supreme Court Chamber on the building's first floor indicates that the stone is in the wall behind it.

When the Architect's office tried to verify the location, it could not locate the stone. The investigation then shifted to the southeast corner of the entire original building, which is in the south (House) wing. There the Architect found a stone in the foundation that he believed to be the missing cornerstone.

The stone was much larger than the stones around it, too large to be just another construction block. Since it was not yet the custom in 1793 to carve any special markings on the stone, the architect could not use such markings to identify the

cornerstone. There were also no traces of the silver plate that was set in place with the cornerstone.

The bronze plaque still hangs in the north wing. In the floor beneath it is a commemorative stone laid in a Masonic ceremony in 1932, the 200th anniversary of Washington's birth. Both mark the wrong location. (The plaque and stone were originally on the exterior of the Capitol, but the 1958-62 extension of the East Front brought them indoors.)

The cornerstone's true location in the south wing is marked only by a plywood cover over the excavation, in a basement corridor near the Capitol coffee shop.

Even though the Architect is satisfied that the block under the coffee shop is the true cornerstone, a mystery still surrounds the discovery: What happened to the silver plate? The Architect's office theorizes that the plate may have been stolen after the ceremony, or lost when the foundations were rebuilt by Latrobe in 1803. Most likely, the plate may have been excavated with dirt and debris when the foundation was strengthened as part of the East Front extension project. Since, at the time, it was generally believed that the stone was located at the other end of the building, no special care was taken to look for or protect the cornerstone or silver plate in the old House wing. The silver plate may have been dug out, hauled away and dumped in a landfill without anyone knowing or suspecting a thing.

The cornerstone laid by President Washington in 1793 was the first of four such ceremonial stones laid at the Capitol, and one of only two whose exact locations are known.

The Capitol's second cornerstone was laid in 1818 to mark the start of construction of the building's center section. This cornerstone was laid without much pageantry, unlike the ceremony 25 years earlier. There was no solemn parade, no artillery salute. The President did not attend; the ceremony was conducted by the Commissioner of

Public Buildings and architect Bulfinch. The second cornerstone was set in the foundation of the center section of the West Front, but its exact location is unknown.

Pomp and ceremony returned to the Capitol when a third cornerstone was laid on July 4, 1851, as work began on the north and south extensions of the building. Following a grand military parade, President Millard Fillmore ceremonially laid the granite stone in place. Architect Walter inserted a jar of coins, documents and other memorabilia into a cavity in the granite stone. Masonic leaders consecrated the stone in a ceremony similar to the one performed by President Washington 58 years earlier. Secretary of State Daniel Webster spoke and an artillery salute followed. The day's events were described as one of the most elaborate ceremonies ever held in the capital. Even so, the precise location of this stone is also lost to history.

It would be exactly 108 years before another cornerstone ceremony would be held at the Capitol. President Dwight D. Eisenhower presided when the cornerstone for the East Front extension was laid on July 4, 1959. Using the same trowel and gavel that President Washington used in 1793, Eisenhower ceremonially spread mortar and tapped the block of Texas red granite into place. A copper box containing memorabilia of the day was inserted into a niche in the stone. The 1959 cornerstone is located below ground level, but its color and the inscription "A.D. 1959" will make it easier to identify if there are any future excavations near the East Front's foundation

2001: The Mylar Cometh

Security concerns following the terrorist attacks of September 11, 2001 brought a new round of modifications to the Capitol complex. Some of the changes were visible, such as the increased number of traffic barriers to protect against truck bombs or other such attacks. Some were less obvious, such as the application of transparent Mylar film to the windows of the Capitol and all the House and Senate office buildings. The Mylar was installed to reduce the danger of flying glass if a bomb exploded in or near one of the buildings.

The Next Century

The next major change for the Capitol is the addition of an underground visitors center. Located under the East Plaza, the center is designed to provide visitors with a comfortable, indoor waiting area for Capitol tours as well as educational exhibits and a secure entry into the Capitol.

Ground was broken for the new center in 2000. Completion is set for 2005.

A commemorative stone, though not officially a cornerstone, was laid in 2000 when ground was broken for the new visitors center. The stone is located in the East Plaza, opposite the center steps.

JUST LIKE GEORGE

President Dwight Eisenhower lays the cornerstone for the East Front extension in 1959, recalling the 1793 ceremony when President Washington laid the cornerstone for the new Capitol.

PHOTO CREDIT:
Library of Congress.
Neg. no. LC-USA7-14988

2
THE SENATE WING

The Senate wing, the part of the original building just north of the dome, was the first part of the Capitol to be built. It opened for business in 1800. In its early years, this part of the Capitol housed the House, the Senate, the Supreme Court, and the Library of Congress. The wing was partially re-built after only six years because of falling plaster, rotting floors and a leaking roof resulting from poor construction. It was heavily damaged when the British burned the Capitol in 1814 and reoc-cupied when restoration was completed in 1819.

Old Supreme Court Chamber

The Supreme Court met in this part of the Capitol from 1800 until 1935. Ironically, the Court was always considered to be a temporary tenant in the Capitol and it was assumed that the Court would eventually move to its own building, one befitting a separate and co-equal branch of government. Few thought it would take 135 years for the Court to realize this goal.

Perhaps the most historic room in the Capitol is the Old Supreme Court Chamber, located on the first floor of the Senate wing. The Senate oc-cupied a two-story chamber in this space from 1800 to 1808. President John Adams delivered his annual message to Congress here on November 22, 1800. On March 4, 1801, Thomas Jefferson was sworn in as our nation's third President in this chamber, and took the oath for his second term here four years later.

The space was later totally rebuilt to include a large chamber for the Senate on the second floor and a smaller chamber for the Supreme Court on the first floor. In 1810, the Senate moved to its new upper chamber, while the Court took posses-sion of the lower chamber.

It was in this lower hall that the Supreme Court made many of the early decisions shaping the role of the Court and the federal government. Daniel Webster established his reputation as an orator here in his arguments defending his alma mater, Dartmouth College, against a New Hampshire law that would have brought the school under state control. In this chamber, John Quincy Adams ar-gued the case for the African refugees who took control of the slave ship *Amistad*. In 1857, the Court, meeting here, ruled that fugitive slave Dredd Scott had to be returned to his master even though he was captured on free soil.

In 1860, after the Senate moved to its larger chamber in the new north wing, the Supreme Court abandoned the lower chamber and moved to the Old Senate Chamber directly above. The lower chamber became a law library, committee room and eventually a storage area, before being restored to its 1810-1860 look for the 1976 American Bicentennial celebration. Many of the pieces now in the room are original from the early 19th Century, including three of the justices' chairs.

Visitors now enter the chamber through the Robing Room where Chief Justice Roger Taney's robe is on display. Busts of four of the first five Chief Justices—John Jay, John Rutledge, Oliver Ellsworth and John Marshall face the bench from the rear of the chamber. Taney's bust is in the Robing Room.

The 1817 plaster relief "Justice" also decorates the chamber's rear wall. The work, by Italian artist Carlo Franzoni, shows a female figure holding scales and a sword. By her feet, an eagle guards law books, while on the other side a winged youth, representing the new American nation, holds a tablet, representing the Constitution. A rising sun completes the work.

(opposite page)

THE HIGH COURT IN THE LOWER CHAMBER

The Supreme Court occupied a chamber on the first floor of the Senate wing from 1810 until 1860. The room was later used as a law library. It was restored to its early 19th Century appearance in the mid-1970's.

PHOTO CREDIT:
Jeff Lesnik

★ ★ ★

NOT-SO-BLIND JUSTICE

A distinctive feature of the plaster relief of Justice in the Old Supreme Court Chamber is sometimes the subject of a popular myth.

As is typical with such representations, Justice is holding a sword in one hand and scales in the other. Unlike other depictions of Justice, this version is not wearing a blindfold.

A popular story associated with the work is that the Italian artist left the blindfold off deliberately because, in his country, the court system held the accused "guilty until proven innocent," unlike the American legal tradition of "innocent until proven guilty."

The truth of the omission is less philosophical. According to the Senate Historian's office, depictions of Justice minus the blindfold were not uncommon in the early 19th Century.

Still, at least in this case, American Justice isn't so blind after all.

★ ★ ★

Corncobs and Columns

In the entryway outside the Old Supreme Court Chamber are six sandstone columns designed by architect B. Henry Latrobe[1]. The capitals, or tops, of the columns, carry a unique design depicting ears of corn. Latrobe wanted to add a distinctly American touch to the Capitol and said his "corncob capitals" as some called them, "obtained for me more applause from Members of Congress than all the works of magnitude or difficulty that surround them."

Latrobe sent one of the capitals to Thomas Jefferson, knowing of Jefferson's interest in architecture. A copy of it is still on display at Monticello, Jefferson's home in Charlottesville, Virginia. This has led many observers to believe

---

1 Latrobe is often identified in history books by his given first name, Benjamin, but scholars familiar with the architect say he never used that name. Instead, he used his middle name, Henry. He signed documents "B. Henry Latrobe," and his friends and family called him "Henry."

that Jefferson had designed the capitals, but they are Latrobe's creation.

When the British invaded Washington in 1814, troops burst through the front door of the north wing into the foyer outside the Supreme Court Chamber. The soldiers set fire to anything and everything in sight. When Latrobe returned to Washington after the war to rebuild the burned out Capitol, he was happy to see that the columns topped with his corncob design survived the fire, and would be around for future generations to enjoy.

★ ★ ★

WHAT HATH GOD WROUGHT?

Before May 24, 1844, the only way to send a message over significant distances was to give it to a messenger who carried it personally or relayed it to other messengers until it finally reached its destination. A demonstration in the Old Supreme Court Chamber changed that and revolutionized long distance communications.

Samuel F.B. Morse invented a device he called the telegraph, *from the Greek words for "far" and "write". Using electrical energy, Morse could tap out coded signals through a copper wire, to be received, decoded and delivered to the message's intended recipient within minutes instead of hours, days or even weeks. The system of dots and dashes Morse devised for his new invention became known as Morse Code.*

Morse gave the first practical demonstration to Congress by sending messages through wires strung within the Capitol. That won him a $30,000 appropriation to test his new device's use for long-distance communication. Morse and his associates strung a wire between Washington and Baltimore. On May 24, 1844, Morse set up his telegraph in the Supreme Court Chamber of the Capitol. With witnesses including Henry Clay and Dolley Madison standing by, Morse tapped out the message suggested by the young daughter of a friend, "What hath God wrought?" A colleague in Baltimore sent the same message in reply. Morse then transmitted the latest news from Washington to Baltimore, and received news of the day's events in Baltimore. Morse and his telegraph wowed the crowd at the Capitol.

Morse's invention came into public view a few days later when the Democratic Party held its nominating convention in Baltimore. Still operating inside the Capitol, Morse was first to receive word that the convention had abandoned incumbent President Martin Van Buren in favor of a dark horse candidate, former Gov. James K. Polk of Tennessee. In just a few seconds, Morse received news which would have taken two hours to reach Washington by train, even longer by coach or horseback.

The telegraph even played a role in the nomination for Vice President. The convention nominated Sen. Silas Wright, Jr. of New York, who happened to be at the Capitol at the time. When Morse received the news, he immediately relayed it to Wright. Wright responded that he did not want the nomination, and Morse immediately sent word of Wright's decision to Baltimore.

When the news reached the convention, no one believed the message could have been sent to Washington and a response received in just a matter of minutes. The convention adjourned for the night so that a committee appointed to offer the nomination to Wright could return from Washington with his reply.

The next morning, when the committee reported to the convention, it confirmed that Wright had refused the nomination and the message received by telegraph the day before was accurate. A group of Wright's friends and supporters crowded into the telegraph office in Baltimore and exchanged messages with the Senator in Washington, trying to convince him to change his mind. They were unsuccessful, and the nomination went to George Dallas of Pennsylvania.

Morse and his associates continued to operate the Washington end of the telegraph line from the Capitol for several months, until control of the system was turned over to the Post Office Department in early 1845.

Telegraph wires eventually crisscrossed the country, connecting the Eastern cities with Texas, California and the rest of the West. The Trans-Atlantic Cable later linked North America with Europe, shrinking the time it took for information to cross the ocean from weeks by ship to seconds by wire.

The telegraph established the scientific principles that later brought us the telephone, radio, television, the Internet and wireless communication, not to mention junk e-mail.

★ ★ ★

The Old Senate Chamber

On the Capitol's second floor, directly above the Old Supreme Court Chamber, is the Old Senate Chamber, home to the U.S. Senate from 1810 to 1859 and to the Supreme Court from 1860 to 1935.

This is the room in which Senators John C. Calhoun of South Carolina, Henry Clay of Kentucky, and Daniel Webster of Massachusetts engaged in their famous debates over slavery and states' rights. Future Presidents Andrew Jackson and Andrew Johnson served here, as well as the future president of the Confederate States of America, Jefferson Davis, and the former president of the Republic of Texas, Sam Houston.

THE OLD SENATE CHAMBER

From 1810 to 1859, the Senate occupied a chamber designed by Latrobe on the second floor of the Capitol. When the Senate moved to its larger quarters in the new wing, the Supreme Court moved into the chamber and occupied it for 75 years. The room is still occasionally used for meetings of the Senate.

⋯ ★ ★ ★ ⋯

MUD AND MODESTY

The red-curtained and carpeted Senate hall had a gallery from which visitors could observe the deliberations of the Senators on the floor of the chamber. The gallery became a popular place with the ladies of Washington who would come down to the Capitol to see and be seen by their social circle. To prevent the Senators on the floor below from catching a glimpse of the frilly petticoats under the ladies' skirts, a "modesty curtain" was hung on the grating to block the view and maintain dignity in the chamber.

Men visiting the gallery created problems of their own. A special sign was posted in the gallery, advising that, "Gentlemen will be pleased not to place their feet on the board in front of the gallery, as the dirt from them falls upon Senator's heads."

⋯ ★ ★ ★ ⋯

By the 1850's, the country, and, consequently, Congress, had outgrown the Capitol's confines and an expansion of the building was necessary. New north and south wings designed by architect Thomas U. Walter were added to the Capitol. The Senate Chamber in the new north wing was ready by 1859. The next year, the Supreme Court moved upstairs to occupy the Old Senate Chamber.

When the Supreme Court moved to its own building across First St. NE in 1935, the Old Senate Chamber became a reception and conference room for Senators. Like the Old Supreme Court Chamber below it, the Old Senate Chamber was restored to its early glory in time for the 1976 Bicentennial. It is still used by the Senate for sessions in which extreme security is in order. In 1999, the chamber served as the jury room for the Senate during the impeachment trial of President Bill Clinton.

The restored chamber contains 64 mahogany desks, all reproductions, since the original furniture moved with the Senate to its new chamber, where many of the pieces are still in use.

The Vice President's desk at the front of the semi-circular room is covered by a mahogany canopy topped with a gilded eagle on a shield. The eagle and shield are original. The canopy is a copy.

Above the canopy is a portrait of George Washington by Rembrandt Peale. Peale first painted the Father of Our Country in 1795, when the artist was only 17. This painting dates to 1824 and is based on Peale's earlier studies of Washington, portraits of Washington by the artist's father, Charles Willson Peale, the famed Washington portraits by Gilbert Stuart and the life sculpture of Washington by Jean Antoine Houdon. The Rembrandt Peale painting is reputed to be the most valuable work of art in the Capitol, but, in reality, the Capitol is filled with many priceless works that could contend for that title.

The Small Senate Rotunda

Between the Old Senate Chamber and the Capitol's main Rotunda is a circular well known as the Small Senate Rotunda. Originally designed as a stairwell, it was reconfigured after the British invasion to bring light from a rooftop skylight to the lower floors. The area above the well has since been closed off.

Now light comes from a beautiful crystal chandelier. Weighing 2,000 lbs., the chandelier contains 150 light bulbs and 14,000 crystals, and has its own colorful history. Although some say the chandelier began life in a brothel, its first home was actually a Baltimore burlesque house called the Maryland Theater. In 1951, the chandelier was purchased by Trinity Methodist Episcopal Church on Capitol Hill in Washington. When the Trinity congregation built a new church in 1964, the Architect of the Capitol purchased the chandelier for $1,500.

The pillars encircling the well are topped with capitals showing the leaves and flowers of the tobacco plant, another Latrobe design, like the corncob capitals, to add a uniquely American feature to the building.

* * *

TAKE MY CHANDELIERS...PLEASE!

When Teddy Roosevelt was President, eight crystal chandeliers graced his office in the White House and the corridor leading to it. Although beautiful to behold, the President ordered them removed. According to one account, Roosevelt couldn't stand the constant tinkling of the crystal ornaments. Another explanation is that the White House was being remodeled and the Victorian chandeliers did not fit the new Georgian decor.

The eight chandeliers were removed to the Capitol. One was returned in 1962 at the request of First Lady Jacqueline Kennedy.

* * *

The Senate Chamber

In 1859, the U.S. Senate moved into its new chamber in the recently constructed north wing of the Capitol, where it has met ever since. In this room, Senators debated the conduct of the Civil War, and every war to follow. They considered the impeachments of two Presidents, and debated the Reconstruction of the South and the extension of civil rights to African Americans. Appointments by every President since James Buchanan for federal offices from the Cabinet to the Supreme Court were deliberated in this room.

The chamber currently holds 100 mahogany Senators' desks arranged in a semi-circle. Republicans sit on the right side of the center aisle (as you face the front of the chamber), Democrats on the left. The two party leaders sit across the aisle from each other in the front row. Other Senators choose their desks and locations within their party's section by seniority. (The back of the room is very popular with senior Senators.) Independents usually choose to sit on the side of the room most appropriate for their political leanings. One Senator, Wayne Morse of Oregon, once had his desk placed in the middle of the center aisle to emphasize his independence.

Nearly half of the Senators' desks date back to 1819, when 48 desks were ordered from cabinet maker Thomas Constantine of New York to replace the desks destroyed in the 1814 fire. New desks of similar design were added as the Senate expanded. Over the years, the desks were modified with writing boxes and shelves added. The desks still hold inkwells and sand shakers dating back to when quill pens were used by the Senators.

BEAUTIFUL LIGHT

An ornate chandelier illuminates the Small Senate Rotunda and the Tobacco Capitals. The chandelier previously hung in a Baltimore theater and a Washington church before coming to the Capitol.

PHOTO CREDIT:
Jeff Lesnik

Ninety-nine of the desks in the Senate Chamber are equipped with flip-top writing boxes. The exception is the desk originally occupied by Webster, who refused to add the flip-top box to his desk. In order to keep a uniform look in the chamber, the Webster desk is elevated to the same height as the rest by placing it on blocks.

A scar from a bayonet distinguishes the desk once occupied by Davis. A Union soldier from Massachusetts, on duty guarding the Capitol during the Civil War, made the mark to show his contempt of Davis, who was then President of the Confederacy. The soldier was admonished by a Senate doorkeeper who told him his job was to protect the Capitol and its contents, not damage or destroy them.

★ ★ ★

SPECIAL DESKS

The desks once occupied by three noted Senators of the early 19th Century—Webster, Davis and Clay—carry with them a special significance.

By tradition and by a rule of the Senate since 1974, the desk originally occupied by Webster is awarded to the senior Senator from New Hampshire. (Webster represented Massachusetts in the House and Senate, but he was born in New Hampshire and first represented that state in the House.)

Webster's desk, or at least its Hollywood stand-in, even played a role in the 1939 Frank Capra film "Mr. Smith Goes to Washington." In the film, newly elected Senator Jeff Smith, played by James Stewart, is led to his seat by a Senate page who tells him that the desk was once used by Webster.

A similar resolution in 1995 reserves the desk used by Davis, who represented Mississippi in the Senate before the Civil War, for the use of the senior Senator from Mississippi.

In 1999, the Senate passed a third such resolution, this one giving the senior Senator from Kentucky first dibs on the desk once used by Clay, the Great Compromiser.

★ ★ ★

SENATE TRADITIONS

The Senate chamber provides each Senator with an individual desk. Forty-eight of the chamber's 100 mahogany desks date back to 1819; the rest were added as states joined the Union. Snuff boxes, inkwells and spitoons, leftovers from an earlier era, still decorate the chamber.

The upper walls of the Senate chamber are lined with busts of the first 20 Vice Presidents of the United States. Busts of later Vice Presidents are displayed outside the chamber.

PHOTO CREDIT:
Library of Congress.

The presiding officer sits at the marble desk at the front of the Senate Chamber, known as the President's Rostrum. Clerks sit at the lower desk in front of the presiding officer. When Senators address the chamber, they stand at their desks, where a clip-on microphone is provided. Clerk typists take down every word, and the transcript is published in the Congressional Record.

Busts of twenty former Vice Presidents line the upper walls of the chamber. Busts of the other Vice Presidents are displayed in the hallways outside the chamber.

A gallery provides the public and news media access to the Senate Chamber to watch the debates. Television cameras were added to the gallery in 1987 to provide continuous coverage of Senate proceedings.

Sweets, Snuff and Spittoons

A Senator with a sweet tooth can indulge his appetite by stopping off at a desk in the rear of the chamber, the official "candy desk."

The tradition started with Sen. George Murphy, a Republican from California, in 1968. Murphy kept a supply of candy in his desk in the last row, near the doors leading to the elevator. Murphy would offer candy to his fellow Senators, and was soon keeping a supply of his colleagues' favorite treats.

His desk became known as the "candy desk," and by tradition, whichever Senator's desk occupies that location must be stocked with candy for the rest of the Senate. The sweet treats are now supplied by the candy manufacturers. Democrats, eventually wearying of having to seek their sweets on the Republican side of the chamber, have started their own candy desk tradition on their side of the room.

Throwbacks to an earlier tradition continue in the form of two lacquered snuff boxes on either side of the President's rostrum of the Senate Chamber. Popular in the 18th and early 19th Centuries, snuff is a powdered form of tobacco that is inhaled through the nose a pinch at a time. Users claimed sniffing snuff would help them ward off colds and clear their heads for debate. The snuff boxes still had a few regular visitors as late as the 1930's. The snuff supply is no longer kept up, and the boxes have been encased in plexiglass.

Also kept for decorative rather than practical use are brass cuspidors, or spittoons. The cuspidors came into use in the 1800's, but, due to some Senators' poor aim, a good deal of tobacco juice still stained the Senate's red carpeting.

NIXON HOLDS UP THE BUST LINE

The tradition of displaying marble busts of former Vice Presidents dates back to 1885 when the Senate decided to honor former Vice President Henry Wilson. The idea was later expanded to honor each former Veep with a bust. Twenty busts line the upper walls of the Senate Chamber. (Wilson's bust is not one of them. More on that later.) Busts of other Vice Presidents are located elsewhere in the Senate wing.

By 1958, the bust collection was complete up to Alben W. Barkley, who served under President Harry S Truman. Next in line was Richard M. Nixon, for his service as Vice President from 1953 to 1961 under Dwight D. Eisenhower. A bust of Nixon was delivered to the Senate in 1967 to less-than-rave reviews and was promptly sent back to the sculptor. The new bust arrived in 1968, while Nixon was running for President. When he won the election, Nixon suggested that the Senate not display his bust until after he left the White House. No one would have predicted at that time that Nixon's presidency would be tainted by the Watergate scandal and he would resign from office in 1974.

Nixon's resignation forced the Senate to face a dilemma: what to do with his Vice Presidential bust? Should the bust be displayed with the other Vice Presidents, as befitting Nixon's eight years in that office? Or should the unprecedented scandal and resignation deny him that privilege?

On top of that, Nixon's first Vice President, Spiro Agnew, had also resigned under the cloud of scandal, and the Senate had to deal with his right to a bust as well.

Nixon's bust eventually came out of storage and was given its place among the other Veeps. Agnew's bust was added in 1995, more than 20 years after he and Nixon resigned from office.

QUESTIONABLE BUSTS

The Watergate scandal of the early 1970's led the Senate to question whether Richard Nixon (top) or Spiro Agnew should be included in the Vice Presidential Bust Collection.

The President's Room

Adjacent to the Senate Chamber is what may be the most ornate room in the Capitol.

The President's Room was included in the design of the new Senate wing with the belief that the President of the United States would pay frequent visits to the Capitol and would need an office in the building. Indeed, Presidents used the room to sign bills into law as late as 1933.

Although occasionally used for Presidential visits, today the President's Room is most commonly used by Senators for meetings and news conferences. It also holds cases displaying many of the diplomatic gifts given to Senators over the years.

The room is decorated with frescoes by the Italian-American artist Constantino Brumidi, whose art decorates much of the Capitol. In 1991, the room's artwork and gilding were restored and historic furnishings were returned to give the room the look it had in the 1870's.

The Vice President's Ceremonial Office

Since the Vice President is the official presiding officer of the Senate, the north wing included an office for the Vice President adjacent to the new Senate Chamber. Although not as ornate as the President's Room, the Vice President's Ceremonial Office is quite striking in its own right. The room is lit by a seven-tiered chandelier that was brought from the White House in 1902.

Since the Vice President seldom attends sessions of the Senate any more, the room is generally used by Senators for meetings.

Vice President Wilson died in this room in 1875. (See the chapter on Ghosts.) A bust of Wilson and his desk are among the room's furnishings. Also in this office, President Chester A. Arthur was sworn in following the death of President James Garfield in 1881.

THE WILSON DESK

After Vice President Wilson died in the Vice President's office in 1875, his desk remained in the room and became known simply as the Wilson Desk.

The desk remained there until 1969, when President Richard Nixon asked that it be moved to the White House so he could use it as his personal desk in the Oval Office. Nixon was familiar with the Wilson Desk from his days as Vice President, but there is evidence that he mistakenly associated the desk with President Woodrow Wilson instead of Vice President Henry Wilson. President Wilson never served as Vice President nor as a Senator and most likely never used the desk.

The Wilson Desk took on new significance when Nixon had it wired with secret microphones and tape recorders in order to record conversations in his office. The tapes played a starring role in the Watergate scandal, which led to Nixon's resignation in 1974.

In 1977, the desk returned to the Vice President's Ceremonial Office. Vice President Walter Mondale, it is said, often crawled under the desk to show visitors where Nixon had hidden the recording devices.

The Senate Reception Room

Just off the Senate floor is the Senate Reception Room. The ornate room, decorated by Brumidi, serves as a convenient place for Senators to meet with constituents and lobbyists without straying too far from debate on the Senate floor. This room was especially useful in the days before the construction of the Senate office buildings across the street from the Capitol.

Brumidi included portraits of George Washington, Thomas Jefferson and Alexander Hamilton in his Reception Room Murals, but left

13 oval panels on the walls of the room for the later addition of portraits of future famous Americans. In 1959, the Senate unveiled portraits of prominent former Senators in five of the spaces. Selected by a special committee headed by Sen. John F. Kennedy, the so-called "Famous Five" consisted of the "Great Triumvirate" of the pre-Civil War days: Calhoun, Clay, and Webster. Joining the triumvirate were two 20th Century Senators: Robert M. LaFollette, Sr., of Wisconsin and Robert Taft of Ohio.

In 2000, the Senate voted to fill two more of the spaces. Selected to join the Famous Five were Arthur H. Vandenburg of Michigan and Robert F. Wagner of New York.

(Read more about the Senate's "Famous Five plus Two" at the end of this chapter.)

The Robert Dole Balcony

On the second floor of the Senate wing, where it connects to the original building, is a private balcony overlooking the National Mall with a spectacular view of the Washington Monument, the Lincoln Memorial, the Smithsonian museums and downtown Washington.

The balcony is adjacent to the office Sen. Robert Dole occupied during his term as Majority Leader. The Kansas Republican enjoyed sitting on the balcony while reviewing papers or meeting with colleagues or staff. When Dole resigned from the Senate in 1996 to seek the Presidency, his colleagues honored him by officially attaching his name to the balcony.

The Ohio Clock

An intricately carved clock called the Ohio Clock adorns the lobby outside the main entrance to the Senate Chamber. Legend has it that the clock was presented to the Senate when Ohio was admitted as the 17th State in 1803. The clock is decorated with a shield containing 17 stars, lending credence to the story.

The truth is that when the clock was ordered and delivered there were 19 states in the union. Nonetheless, the clock's association with Ohio has stuck.

★ ★ ★

HIDEAWAYS

Scattered throughout the Senate wing are more than 90 private offices or "hideaways" for Senators' use. The hideaway offices are convenient refuges for Senators to hold a private meeting, make a confidential phone call or even grab a nap during a late session without having to return to their offices across the street in the Senate office buildings.

Hideaways vary in size and amenities. Some are highly coveted, but many are cramped, windowless rooms with space for little more than a desk and a sofa. Nonetheless, a hideaway is one of the most cherished perks in the Senate.

★ ★ ★

GOOD RECEPTION

The ornate Senate Reception Room was designed by Constantino Brumidi. Portraits in special wall panels honor seven Senators of years past.

PHOTO CREDIT:
Library of Congress
Neg. no. LC-USA7-33805

Minton Tiles

A distinctive difference between the old and new Senate and House wings of the Capitol is right under the visitor's nose. Actually, it's also under the visitor's feet.

Latrobe used paving stones for the flooring in the corridors and public spaces of the original Capitol building. He used brick for the offices and committee rooms.

Walter wanted something more distinctive for the corridors of the new Senate wing. Yet, the flooring also had to be durable. He chose encaustic tiles manufactured by Minton, Hollins and Co. of Stoke-on-Trent, England. The colorful tiles were installed to form beautiful patterns in the floor. Approximately 1,000 different patterns are employed in the Minton corridors.

The Minton tiles proved to be very durable, the colorful patterns surviving underfoot for more than 100 years. Still, by the 1970's, the tiles had begun to show wear. The Architect of the Capitol began looking for replacement tiles, but none could match the combination of color and durability of the original Mintons.

The Architect eventually found H & R Johnson Co., also of Stoke-on-Trent. The Johnson firm was the successor to Minton, Hollins and Co. and still had records of the tiles made for the Capitol more than a century earlier. Johnson Co. officials were reluctant to try to resurrect a 19th Century tile-making process to create a product for which there would be such a limited market. When they discovered that the British Parliament and the Smithsonian Institution also had some Minton tiles to re-place, the company saw a future in the old Minton process.

The architect began replacing the worn Minton tiles with the new ones from H & R Johnson in 1986.

The Battle of Lake Erie

Hanging above a landing on the Senate wing's east staircase is William Henry Powell's striking oil painting, *The Battle of Lake Erie*. The 20-by-30-foot canvas shows Oliver Hazard Perry, commander of the American Fleet, transferring command from his damaged flagship, the *U.S.S. Lawrence*, to the *U.S.S. Niagara* during the battle of September 10, 1813. Despite early setbacks, Perry was able to turn the tide of the battle and defeat the British fleet. In perhaps the most significant naval battle of the War of 1812, Perry's victory secured American control of the Great Lakes.

Powell (1823-1879) completed the work in 1873. Another Powell work, *Discovery of the Mississippi by DeSoto, A.D. 1541* (1855), hangs in the Rotunda.

The Battle of Lake Erie is the subject of two popular myths. One myth holds that the frame of the painting came from one of Perry's ships. The truth is that the U.S. Navy scuttled the vessels at the end of the war, 58 years before Powell created the painting. The other myth purports that all the sailors in Perry's boat are based on the same model (or are even self-portraits of the artist.) Not true. Powell used actual sailors from the Brooklyn Navy Yard as models. Powell enlarged the eyes of the figures for his own artistic purposes, but the larger eyes made the men look similar.

In 1955, vandals tore a U-shaped hole in the canvas. The tear measured 11 inches high and nine inches wide. Officials said the size and location of the tear led them to believe it was caused by a heavy object, such as a book, being thrown at the painting.

Repairs cost $22,500.

The Recall of Columbus

Christopher Columbus had an idea. The navigator from Genoa thought he could reach India and China by sailing west from Europe. For centuries, traders had been traveling overland to these exotic places. In Columbus' day, sailors were beginning to map a sea route by rounding the southern tip of Africa. Still, Columbus insisted his plan would be the safest, cheapest and most direct route. All he needed was money.

Columbus pitched his idea to King Ferdinand and Queen Isabella of Spain, but they balked at the cost. Columbus was on his way to present his idea to the King of France when he was stopped near Grenada by a messenger from the Spanish court. The King and Queen had reconsidered his proposal and would bankroll his expedition.

The 1882 painting, *The Recall of Columbus* by Augustus G. Heaton, shows this important turning point in Columbus' journey to the Americas. It hangs in a third floor corridor in the Senate wing.

The First Reading of the Emancipation Proclamation

Artist Francis Bicknell Carpenter spent six months at the White House in 1864 to recreate the scene of President Lincoln and his Cabinet at the first reading of the Emancipation Proclamation.

Carpenter asked his subjects to position themselves around the table in the President's office as they had been during the actual first reading a year earlier. In creating his work, though, Carpenter rearranged the men so that Lincoln is flanked by the two factions of his cabinet, those who fully endorsed the Proclamation, and those who, at least at first, displayed doubt or opposition to it.

Lincoln is shown seated at the head of the table, facing Secretary of State William Seward, with Secretary of War Edwin Stanton and Treasury Secretary Salmon P. Chase to the President's approximate right. To Lincoln's left are Secretary of the Navy Gideon Welles, Secretary of the Interior Caleb B. Smith, Postmaster General Montgomery Blair, and Attorney General Edward Bates.

The artist included a bust of Simon Cameron, the man who placed Lincoln's name in nomination for President, in the far left of the painting. A portrait of Andrew Jackson is nearly invisible in the background.

Carpenter's painting, which hangs over the west staircase near the Senate Chamber, was displayed at the White House and the Capitol, then toured the country before it was purchased in 1877 by Elizabeth Thompson of New York for $25,000. Ms. Thompson donated the work as a gift to the nation on February 12, Lincoln's birthday, the following year.

Space for the Space Age

On the first floor of the Senate wing are the Brumidi Corridors. Decorated with ornate patterns and scenes from history, the corridors are inspired by Raphael's work at the Vatican. While many artists did the actual paintings, Brumidi created the designs and supervised the work.

Brumidi created frescoes of allegorical portrayals or important scenes from American history in the semi-circular areas—*lunettes*—over doorways. Brumidi expected great things from America, and left spaces in his corridors for those accomplishments to be recorded. An unknown artist added two landmark events in aviation—the Wright Brothers' first flight in 1903 and Charles Lindbergh's 1927 non-stop flight across the Atlantic.

In 1975, Allyn B. Cox, whose work decorates the House wing, was commissioned to commemorate the 1969 moon landing. The painting shows

SPACE AGE ART

Panels commemorating the Apollo 11 moon landing and honoring the seven astronauts who died in the explosion of the space shuttle *Challenger* are two recent additions to the Brumidi corridor on the first floor of the Senate wing.

PHOTO CREDIT:
Jeff Lesnik

A bust of the artist Constantino Brumidi stands among his frescoes in the Senate wing of the Capitol.

PHOTO CREDIT:
Jim Berard

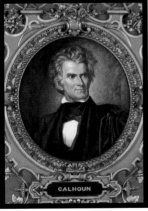

JOHN C. CALHOUN
By Arthur E, Schmalz Conrad

PHOTO CREDIT:
U.S. Senate Collection
Cat. no. 32-00009-000

astronauts Neil Armstrong and Edwin Aldrin raising the American flag on the moon. The latest addition to the Brumidi Corridors is a tribute to the seven astronauts, including teacher Christa McAuliffe, lost in the 1986 *Challenger* explosion. It was painted in 1987 by Charles Schmidt.

THE MICHELANGELO OF THE CAPITOL

Constantino Brumidi was nearly 50 years old and one of the most respected artists in Rome when he emigrated to the United States in 1852. Brumidi was proud to be in America and his artwork reflected his hope for a bright future for his adopted country. He decorated the new extensions of the Capitol and the inner dome with art that blended the classical styles he studied in Italy with figures and designs that are truly American. He made great use of the fresco *technique, which involves adding pigment to drying plaster, creating a work of art much more enduring than one simply painted on top of the dried surface.*

He has been dubbed "The Michelangelo of the Capitol," but perhaps the best description of Brumidi is the one he chose for himself when he signed one of his frescoes, "C. Brumidi Artist Citizen of the U.S."

The Famous Five, Plus Two

Here is some background on the seven men honored with portraits in the Senate Reception Room:

John C. Calhoun, South Carolina (1782-1850)
House of Representatives 1811-1817
Vice-President 1825-1832
Senate 1832-1843, 1846-1850

A staunch supporter of Southern rights, John C. Calhoun had an illustrious career spanning nearly 40 years in Washington. Calhoun served six years in the House, and a total of 16 years in the Senate. Interspersed among his Congressional terms, he served as Secretary of War under President James Monroe, Secretary of State under President John Tyler, and Vice President under two consecutive Presidents, John Quincy Adams and Andrew Jackson.

Calhoun was the leading voice in Congress in favor of the sovereign rights of the states and against the abolition of slavery. He often faced off with contemporaries Henry Clay and Daniel Webster on these issues.

He was also the author of the gag rule that prohibited Congress from debating the slavery issue, a rule John Quincy Adams worked hard to abolish.

Calhoun's philosophies defined the Southern position that led to the Civil War.

Henry Clay, Kentucky (1777-1852)
Senate 1806-1807, 1810-1811, 1831-1842, 1849-1852
House of Representatives 1811-1814, 1815-1821, 1823-1825
Speaker of the House 1811-1814, 1815-1820, 1823-1825

One of the greatest legislators ever to serve in Congress, Henry Clay actually began his Congressional career in violation of the U.S. Constitution. A member of the Kentucky House of Representatives, Clay was elected to the Senate in 1806. At age 29, he was one year shy of the Constitutional minimum age of 30 for Senators. He only served four months before returning to the state legislature.

Clay returned to Washington and the Senate in 1810 to fill another vacancy. This time he served 14 months. In the meantime, he was elected to the House of Representatives, where he served from 1811 to 1814. Clay was elected Speaker of the House in his first term. He was 34 years old at the time and is the youngest person to hold the post of Speaker. Clay was elected to five more terms in the House, four of them as Speaker between 1815 and 1825.

In the Presidential election of 1824, Clay was one of four candidates in a field that also included Andrew Jackson and John Quincy Adams. When the Electoral College failed to give any candidate a majority, the election was turned over to the House of Representatives. The House, with Clay as Speaker, gave the Presidency to Adams. Clay later resigned from the House to serve as Adams' Secretary of State. Jackson accused Clay of fixing the House vote in favor of Adams in exchange for the job, and never forgave Clay for that.

Clay would run for President three more times, all unsuccessfully, but would make his reputation in the U.S. Senate.

In 1831, Clay was elected to the Senate for the third time, yet again to fill a vacancy. He was elected to a full term in 1836 and served until 1842. After his fourth and final run for the Presidency in 1844, Clay once again returned to the Senate and served until his death in 1852.

As the Civil War neared, Clay became the voice of compromise in the Senate. Often caught between the Northern rhetoric of Webster and the Southern fire of Calhoun, Clay worked to forge agreements to hold the fledgling union together. He was the architect of the Compromise of 1850, which allowed California to enter the Union as a free state and ended the slave trade—but not slavery itself—in the District of Columbia. To assuage the Southern Senators, the compromise also toughened the Fugitive Slave Act.

Clay's compromise, as brilliantly crafted and negotiated as it was, only postponed the inevitable. In 1861, eleven years after the compromise and nine years after Clay's death, Southern states seceded from the Union, and the Civil War began.

Robert M. La Follette, Sr., Wisconsin
(1855-1925)
House of Representatives 1885-1891
Senate 1906-1925

A former U.S. Representative and Governor of Wisconsin (1901-1906), Robert Marion La Follette was elected to the Senate in 1904, but delayed his assumption of the seat until he finished his term as Governor.

In the Senate, La Follette became the nucleus of a group of independent Republicans looking to reform the institution and break the hold lobbyists had on the Senate.

From the nation's beginning, special interests sent lobbyists—agents whose job it was to try to influence the actions of Congress—to persuade Senators and Reprsentatives on important issues. The lobbyists used food and drink, even prostitutes and bribery to build support on key issues. Gun maker Samuel Colt is said to have handed out pistols to Members of Congress to gain an extension on his patent.

By La Follette's time, the fiercest lobbying took place over tariff issues. In the years before the nation levied an income tax on individuals or corporations, the prime source of revenue for the federal government was the imposition of tariffs on imported goods. The tariffs could also be used to protect domestic industries from cheaper imports. Industries facing foreign competition wanted tariffs raised, shipping interests and industries depending on imported raw materials wanted them lowered. A small adjustment in a tariff could mean millions of dollars to a large company.

La Follette became the chief adversary of fellow Republican Sen. Nelson Aldrich of Rhode Island. Aldrich chaired the Republican Conference and determined committee assignments. He also chaired the Senate Finance Committee, which had jurisdiction over federal taxes and tariffs. Aldrich was considered the most

powerful man in the Senate at that time, and saw no need to change or abandon the tariff system. Senators receiving generous favors from industrial lobbyists agreed.

La Follette stopped the gravy train when, before a vote on a new tariff bill, he called upon his fellow Senators to disclose their stock holdings and business interests.

Public disclosure of financial holdings is now required of all Senators and Representatives.

La Follette ran for President on the Progressive Party ticket in 1924. He came in third.

Sen. Robert Byrd of West Virginia, in his 1989 history of the Senate, wrote that "La Follette preferred to go down fighting for a deeply felt cause than to accept partial victory through compromise."

Robert A. Taft, Ohio (1889-1953)
Senate 1939-1953

In his Pulitzer Prize-winning book *Profiles in Courage*, John F. Kennedy wrote, "The late Robert A. Taft of Ohio was never President of the United States. Therein lies his personal tragedy. And therein lies his national greatness."

Taft was the son of former President and Chief Justice William Howard Taft. His goal in public life was to follow in his father's footsteps and serve in the White House. The leading Republican of his time, Robert Taft tried three times for his party's Presidential nomination. Three times he was denied.

Taft was a man of conscience who refused to compromise his principles for political gains—or to avoid political penalties. Representing Ohio, a heavily industrialized and unionized state, Taft was co-author of the Taft-Hartley Labor Relations Act of 1947, which significantly limited union power. At the end of World War II, Taft questioned the death sentences handed down to Nazi war criminals at the Nuremberg trials. Taft did not question the guilt of the accused, nor the appalling atrocities they committed. His concern stemmed from the fact that he did not believe there was sufficient pre-existing legal authority to impose such a penalty. He felt the sentences were handed down on legal bases established *ex post facto* (after the deed), which is prohibited by the U.S. Constitution. If Americans are to believe in individual rights and liberties, Taft supposed, we should extend those principles to the international arena rather than abandon them.

Such an unpopular position—though legally and morally sound—inhibited Taft's ability to build a national constituency and ascend to the Presidency.

In 1959, a memorial carillon dedicated to Robert A. Taft was erected in Senate Park, north of the Capitol. It is the only such memorial to a U.S. Senator on the Capitol grounds.

Arthur H. Vandenburg, Michigan (1884-1951)
Senate 1928-1951

Arthur H. Vandenberg's early years in the Senate were marked by his staunch opposition to American involvement in foreign conflict. After the attack on Pearl Harbor brought the war to America, Vandenburg's views changed. By the end of the war, he had become an internationalist. As the chairman of the Senate Foreign Relations Committee, Vandenburg, a Republican, was a leading advocate of Democratic President Harry S. Truman's programs for rebuilding Europe and Japan, and creating a North Atlantic alliance to contain the growing influence of the Soviet Union.

ROBERT A. TAFT
By Deane Keller

Robert F. Wagner, New York
Senate 1927-1949

A contemporary of Vandenburg, Robert F. Wagner's greatest contribution was in domestic affairs, particularly the rights of working men and women. He was the lead sponsor of two of the most far-reaching legislative initiatives of the 1930's: the Social Security Act and the Wagner Labor Act, which guaranteed workers the right to organize into unions and bargain collectively with their employers.

Daniel Webster, New Hampshire and Massachusetts
House of Representatives 1813-1817, 1823-1827
Senate 1827-1841, 1845-1850

One of the most eloquent speakers to grace the halls of the Capitol was Daniel Webster. Born in New Hampshire, Webster served two terms in Congress before moving to Boston in 1816. He made a national name for himself defending his alma mater, Dartmouth College, in a case before the U.S. Supreme Court. He later returned to Congress representing Massachusetts in the House (1823-1827) and in the Senate (1827-1841, 1845-1850). Webster also served as Secretary of State under Presidents William Henry Harrison and John Tyler (1841-1843) and President Millard Fillmore (1850-1852).

Perhaps Webster's finest moment came on March 7, 1850, when he delivered his famous speech in favor of a compromise he and Clay had worked out in the preceding weeks. Clay knew the compromise could not succeed without the support of Webster, the leading voice of the North. Webster agreed to Clay's compromise, and on that Seventh of March, rose to defend it.

"I wish to speak today, not as a Massachusetts man, nor a Northern man, but as an American," Webster began.

Webster spoke for more than three hours to a packed Senate Chamber. The audience included Representatives, diplomats, and many individual- who had traveled for days to witness the speech. It also included the aged and ailing Calhoun, who was so weak that he had to be helped to his seat.

Webster's words were not in support of abolition or in defense of slavery. He told his colleagues that the Senate had to be most concerned with preservation of the Union. And he warned them that the Union would not survive unless this compromise was forged.

Webster won the argument. Congress adopted the Compromise of 1850 and Clay was hailed as its author. Webster, on the other hand, was widely condemned by his former allies in the North as a traitor for his support of the pro-Southern points of the plan.

Webster resigned from the Senate four months later to serve the final two years of his life as Secretary of State.

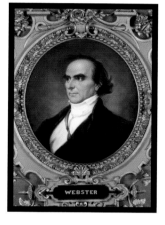

DANIEL WEBSTER
By Adrian S. Lamb

PHOTO CREDIT:
U.S. Senate Collection
Cat. no. 32-00006-000

3

THE HOUSE WING

During its first seven years in Washington, after moving south from Philadelphia in 1800, the House of Representatives met for a short time in the Senate wing, and later in a low, round building nicknamed The Oven. The House wing was the second section of the original Capitol building to be completed. The House moved into its new quarters in 1807.

The House had barely settled in when, in 1814, British invaders torched the Capitol. Architects B. Henry Latrobe and Charles Bulfinch supervised the rebuilding of the wing, which the Representatives reoccupied in 1819.

By the 1850's, Congress outgrew the original confines of the Capitol. A new extension was added to the House wing. The addition included a new, larger chamber for the House of Representatives. In 1857, the House convened in its new chamber, where it continues to meet today.

National Statuary Hall (Old House Chamber)

The original House Chamber is a semi-circular, half-domed room on the second floor of the old House wing. Historic, often raucous debates took place on its floor. Henry Clay, Daniel Webster, and John C. Calhoun, who would later become the Senate's "Great Triumvirate", all served here. Future Presidents John Tyler, Millard Fillmore, James K. Polk, Franklin Pierce, James Buchanan and Abraham Lincoln also served in this chamber. So did Davy Crockett and Sam Houston.

Presidents James Madison, James Monroe, and Andrew Jackson were inaugurated in this room. Fillmore took the Presidential oath of office here following the death of Zachary Taylor.

John Quincy Adams, the sixth President of the United States, was sworn in as President, served as a Member of Congress for 17 years, suffered a fatal stroke and had his funeral all in this chamber.

An example of Greek revival architecture, the hall resembles a classical theater.

On the front wall, above where the Speaker's desk once stood, is a statue of Liberty holding a copy of the U.S. Constitution. To Liberty's left is an American eagle, to her right, a serpent, symbolizing wisdom. The work was done in plaster by artist Enrico Causici and placed in the chamber about the time Congress reoccupied the room in 1819.

At the rear of the chamber is a brass clock embedded in a marble statue of History by Carlo Franzoni. The statue depicts the allegorical figure of Clio, the Muse of History, standing in a winged chariot, keeping a written record of the actions of the House with quill and parchment. The chariot sits on a marble globe displaying the signs of the Zodiac. The clock face is formed by the wheel of the chariot. It was installed in 1819.

Old Man Eloquent

No one is more closely associated with this chamber than John Quincy Adams, the sixth President of the United States. "Old Man Eloquent," as he was known, served here for 17 years after he left the White House. He is the only former President to serve in the House of Representatives.

A strong voice for the abolition of slavery, Adams fought bitterly against a gag rule that prevented the House from debating the slavery issue. A masterful legislator, Adams continued to pick away at the gag rule until he succeeded in getting it overturned.

On February 23, 1848, Adams suffered a stroke on the floor of the House. He was taken to the

Speaker's office adjacent to the chamber, where he died a short time later. The room is now a lounge for female Members of Congress.

A bust of Adams is on display in the room where he died. Also in the room is a horsehair sofa purported to be one on which he died. (A twin of this sofa is held by the Supreme Court, and some say that sofa is the one on which Adams died. There is really no way to know for sure which sofa is the genuine article.)

National Statuary Hall

After the House moved to its new hall, the old House chamber stood empty and forlorn for several years. It became a haven for vendors looking to sell their wares to Congressmen passing through the old hall. Rep. Robert C. Schenk of Ohio saw a need to restore some dignity to the old chamber. In 1864 he told the House:

"I never pass through the old hall without feeling myself reproached by the spirits that haunt the place. I look where venerable John Quincy Adams trembled in his seat and voted and I see a huckster woman selling gingerbread. I look where Calhoun and Clay sat...and I find a woman selling oranges and root beer. I look around where men stood and uttered their patriotic sentiments in the days when such sentiments were heard to reverberate everywhere and by every man and I find a floor rotting and trembling beneath my tread."

Rep. Justin S. Morrill of Vermont introduced a bill to convert the empty chamber to a National Statuary Hall where, in Morrill's words, "those who will be here to aid in carrying on the government may daily receive fresh inspiration and new incentives and see the actual form and mold of those who have inerasably fixed their names on the pages of history."

Morrill's bill passed on July 2, 1864 and was signed into law by President Lincoln. On Feb. 3, 1865 Secretary of State William H. Seward sent notice to the governors of the 36 states requesting statues for the new collection. The first statues arrived in 1870. By 1933, the collection had grown so large that Congress, worried about the effects of the heavy statues on the floor of the hall and the aesthetics of having so many statues crammed into the space, authorized the statues to be displayed throughout the building. Today the National Statuary Collection includes 97 statues from all 50 states. (Forty-seven states have donated the maximum two statues; three have donated just one.) Thirty-eight of the statues are currently displayed in Statuary Hall.

Statuary Hall was partially restored to its early 19th Century appearance in 1976 for the Bicentennial celebration. The restoration was based on an oil painting by Samuel F. B. Morse, inventor of the telegraph. Brass plaques mark the places where future Presidents—and one former President—once had their desks.

Twenty columns of Potomac pebblestone surround Statuary Hall and support its half-dome ceiling. In restoring the chamber, workers faced a problem with replicas of the whale oil lamps that once hung from the columns and illuminated the room. The original oil lamps held their own reservoirs and were easily attached to the columns. The replicas, however, were lighted by electricity, and a way had to be found to run power to the lamps without either damaging the columns or running obvious, unsightly wires along them.

The workers employed a low-voltage electrical tape, similar to that used in alarm systems. Electricians ran the tape down the back of each column and around to the lamp replica on the front of the column. Painters then decorated the tape to blend in with the pebblestone, and the power source was rendered nearly invisible to the unsuspecting eye.

Today, Statuary Hall is used for special occasions. After each Inaugural ceremony, the President attends a special luncheon with Congressional leaders in this room. When the President speaks to a joint session of Congress, such as the annual State of the Union address, Statuary Hall is the stake-out position for reporters. The networks as well as individual stations from around the country set up camera positions in the hall and fight to interview Senators and Representatives leaving the House Chamber after the speech.

———————— ★ ★ ★ ————————

THE WHISPERING SPOT

National Statuary Hall, the old House Chamber, has always been plagued with quirky acoustics. The echoes off the half-domed ceiling made debates in the chamber difficult to follow and led, along with the need for more room, to the House's decision in 1850 to build an extension onto the Capitol for a new chamber.

The unique acoustics of this room have made it a favorite with Capitol visitors and may have played a significant role in the early deliberations of the House. Guides love to demonstrate how a person speaking in a normal voice at a particular spot near the front of the chamber can be heard clearly by someone standing in a corresponding spot on the other side of the room.

According to legend, John Quincy Adams, the leader of the Whig party in the House, used this strange phenomenon to his political advantage. Adams' desk was located at the very spot where listeners stand today to hear the whispering demonstration. The speaker giving the demonstration stands near the spot where the Democratic floor leader sat in Adams' day. According to some accounts, Adams, an old man by the time he served in the House, would sit at his desk and pretend to be asleep, all the while listening in on the conversations going on across the room. The Democrats never caught on and were always amazed at Adams' ability to anticipate their legislative moves.

In truth, Adams likely didn't use the effect, or even know about it. The old House Chamber was a boisterous place when Congress was in session there. Acoustics were so bad in the hall that Members had to crowd to the front of the room to hear and participate in debates. It is unlikely that such echoing whispers could be discerned over the cacophony that characterized the chamber in Adams' day. Also the room had a sunken floor with wooden risers when the House met there, not the flat, tile floor of today, so it's unlikely that sound waves would have followed the same path around the room in Adams' time that they do today.

But, whether Adams used it or not, the acoustic phenomenon of the whispering spot really does exist today.

———————— ★ ★ ★ ————————

The House Chamber

Today's House Chamber is a stately hall of walnut panels, leather seats and rich blue carpeting.

The President delivers his annual State of the Union Address in this hall. President Franklin Roosevelt spoke here on December 8, 1941, seeking a declaration of war against Japan for the attack on Pearl Harbor. World leaders such as Winston Churchill and Lech Walesa addressed Congress assembled in this chamber. Nine future Presidents served here, including James Garfield, John F. Kennedy, Richard Nixon and Gerald Ford. Two Presidents, Andrew Johnson and Bill Clinton, were impeached here.

Because of its capacity, the House Chamber is used for joint sessions of Congress. The chamber provides theater-style seating for 450 on the main floor. Extra seating is brought in for Presidential addresses, which are attended by the full House and Senate, as well as the Justices of the Supreme Court, the President's Cabinet and the foreign diplomatic corps. The chamber is surrounded by a visitors gallery.

It took a while for the House to settle on the current seating arrangement in its chamber. When the Representatives moved to their new addition in 1857, the new chamber was outfitted with ornate desks of carved oak. Thanks to the chamber's larger size, Members wanted additional elbow room. The desks were arranged so each Member had space enough to walk completely around his desk. However, in the days before electronic amplification, speakers had a difficult time being heard by the Members of the House spread throughout the larger hall. In 1859, the desks were removed in favor of benches in order to bring the Members closer together.

The new seating scheme lasted just one year. In 1860, the House brought back the desks and donated the benches to the U.S. Court of Claims and St. Elizabeth's hospital in Washington. (Some of the benches were later returned and now serve as seating for tired tourists in the Capitol Rotunda.)

In 1873, the House installed new desks in a more compact arrangement, and in 1902 tried desks in solid sections for even more efficient use of space.

Finally, in 1913, the House came up with its current arrangement. It installed 450 seats in a semicircular pattern on the tiered floor. Since the new theater-like seats did not allow for writing surfaces, four tables were installed in the fourth row for use by party leaders and the managers of the legislation being debated.

* * *

PSST! HEY, BUDDY!
WANNA BUY A CONGRESSIONAL SEAT?

Congressional seats for sale? Legally? It happened in 1951.

The Architect of the Capitol was remodeling the House Chamber and had hundreds of the chamber's old chairs in temporary storage in the Rotunda. So, they were put up for sale.

The Architect's office advertised for bids on the chairs.

There were no takers.

The seats were offered for sale to individual Members. Several expressed interest, but never removed their selections.

They were offered to other government agencies.

No sale.

So, the chairs went on sale to the general public.

What may have hurt sales is the fact that the chairs could not be bought individually. Instead, they were in solid, curved rows of six to 16 seats each, 35 to 50 feet in length.

* * *

Unlike the Senate, the House does not have assigned seats. Members may sit wherever they please, although Republicans generally sit on the right side of the chamber as you face the Speaker, and Democrats generally sit to the left.

When Members wish to speak, they must move to a microphone position, now that the House is wired for sound. The microphones are at the managers' tables in the fourth row and at two lecterns at the front of the chamber—also known as the Well of the House.

The three-tiered Speaker's Podium is at the very front of the hall. The first tier desk provides a work area for clerks keeping track of the business before the House. The second, middle, tier provides a speaking platform for the Bill Reading Clerk, who must read aloud the legislation to be considered. The top tier, in front of a large American flag, is where the Speaker or his designated Speaker Pro Tem sit and preside over the business of the House. (For joint sessions of Congress, a second chair is placed on the top tier for the Vice President or the President Pro Tem of the Senate.)

To the left of the Speaker's Podium, as you face the front of the chamber, is a portrait of George Washington by John Vanderlyn, commissioned by Congress in 1832. Across the room is an 1825 portrait of the Marquis de Lafayette, Washington's friend and ally during the American Revolution, by artist Ary Scheffer.

The Congressional Mace

The Mace is the symbol of authority in the House of Representatives. It is brought into the chamber when the House convenes and is placed on a pedestal to the Speaker's right.

The Mace also signals the rules of procedure in effect on the House floor. When the House is in session, the Mace is in full view on its pedestal. When the House meets as the Committee of the Whole, which allows the body to proceed under less strict rules of debate, the Mace is placed in a holder on the floor at the base of the pedestal.

Historically, the Mace has also been used to keep order. On occasions when the House has become exceptionally unruly, the Speaker has ordered the Mace to be displayed in front of the disorderly Members to remind them of the serious business at hand and the need for decorum.

The current Mace dates back to 1847. It consists of a bundle of ebony rods bound with silver bands and topped with a silver globe and eagle. The first Mace was destroyed when the British burned the Capitol in 1814. A wooden replica replaced it until the current Mace was commissioned.

Voting

When a recorded vote is called in the House, Members vote electronically. The electronic voting system was installed in 1973. Voting stations are located throughout the hall, mounted on the backs of selected seats along the aisles. Members vote by inserting a plastic card, similar to an ATM or debit card, and pressing the button corresponding to their vote on the issue. The buttons are color coded: green for yes, red for no, yellow for abstain or present. The yellow button is also used for Members to respond when attendance is required but there is no vote pending.

When a vote is under way, a scoreboard lights up in the gallery above the Speaker's chair. The board lists each Member by name and indicates how he or she voted by displaying a red, green or yellow dot. Auxiliary boards on the facing of the gallery show the bill number, a running total of votes cast for and against, and the time remaining for Members to cast their votes.

Television cameras, installed in 1979, are mounted in the gallery and record all the business conducted on the House floor. The video is distributed throughout the Capitol and House office buildings on the House cable system, enabling Members and staff to keep track of House proceedings from their offices. The signal is also made available to the news media and the general public may purchase video recordings of debates. C-SPAN retransmits the House TV signal to cable-TV systems throughout the country.

HOUSE MODERN

The modern House chamber includes an elecronic voting system installed in 1973. TV cameras were added in 1979

PHOTO CREDIT:
Library of Congress
Neg. no. LC-USA7-36845

C-SPAN

The installation of television cameras in the House Chamber in 1979 coincided with the birth of what has become an American institution: the Cable-Satellite Public Affairs Network, better known as C-SPAN.

From its inception, a staple of C-SPAN's programming has been gavel-to-gavel coverage of the meetings of the House of Representatives. When the Senate added cameras and began televising its deliberations, C-SPAN added a second network, C-SPAN 2, to carry the Senate coverage. (The House and Senate each operates its own cameras and provides the feed to C-SPAN.)

Despite its coverage of Congress, C-SPAN is not a government agency, nor does it receive any government funding. C-SPAN was created as a public service by the nation's cable-TV operators. It continues to receive its operating funds from subscription fees paid by cable providers.

C-SPAN supplements the House and Senate sessions with call-in shows and coverage of committee hearings, news conferences and other events. As media critic and political commentator Jeff Greenfield wrote, "C-SPAN relies on a blend of modern technology and a Jeffersonian faith in the people. Using lightweight video equipment and reasonably priced satellite time, C-SPAN simply shows up at a political event, turns on the cameras, and lets the viewer see what is happening."

C-SPAN has since added three other outlets: C-SPAN 3, C-SPAN Radio, and the Internet service, C-SPAN.org.

★ ★ ★

OLD LAWMAKER

Moses is one of 23 historic lawgivers represented in marble relief medallions on the upper walls of the House chamber

PHOTO CREDIT:
Architect of the Capitol
Neg. no. 34076

Historic Lawmakers

The upper wall of the House Chamber is decorated with the faces of 23 lawgivers from ancient and modern history. The honorees include Moses, King Hammurabi I of Mesopotamia, Emperor Justinian of Rome, British jurist William Blackstone, and Emperor Napoleon I of France. Two Americans are included: Thomas Jefferson, author of the Declaration of Independence, and George Mason, the Father of the Bill of Rights.

The lawgivers' likenesses are carved in relief on discs of white marble. Each disc is 28 inches in diameter.

At least one modern lawmaker was not satisfied with only two Americans represented in the collection. In 1951, Rep. John Rankin of Mississippi complained that all non-Americans, except Moses, should be replaced with American statesmen. The Southern Congressman recommended fellow Mississippian Jefferson Davis and Virginian Robert E. Lee.

Cloakrooms

Democratic and Republican cloakrooms are located under the gallery in the rear corners of the chamber. The cloakrooms, once used as a place for Members to hang their coats, provide informal space for Members to relax off the floor. The cloakrooms provide casual seating as well as telephones and light refreshments. The staff of the cloakrooms also provide message services for Members and provide information on the House schedule and activities on the House floor.

Speaker's Lobby

The Speaker's Lobby is adjacent to the House Chamber through the doors on either side of the Speaker's podium. It is a place for Members to meet informally with each other or with reporters. Portraits of former Speakers line the walls of the lobby.

An ornate reading room off the lobby provides newspapers and wire service machines to allow Members to keep up with the latest news.

Rayburn Room

Located between the House floor and the Speaker's offices, the Rayburn Room is a reception area where Members of Congress can meet with staff, constituents, lobbyists and others without having to return to their offices. The room is located in part of the East Front extension of the Capitol and named after Sam Rayburn of Texas, who was Speaker of the House when the extension was built.

President Washington

The adoption of the U.S. Constitution is the subject of an oil painting by artist Howard Chandler Christy. The work shows the Constitutional Convention meeting in Philadelphia in 1787. Benjamin Franklin, and James Madison are among the convention delegates represented in the painting. It hangs over the east grand staircase in the House.

Shown standing at the front of the hall is George Washington, president of the convention. Washington's presence gave the delegates a model for the new office of President of the United States. Washington was generally considered the likely choice for the first President under the new Constitution. As the convention drafted language to define the powers and responsibilities of the President, they had Washington himself standing in front of them. In effect, the delegates were deciding what powers and responsibilities they could entrust to Washington. Washington became for the delegates the embodiment of the office of President.

The work was damaged by a vicious act of vandalism in 1966. A 27-year-old man from Patter-son, New Jersey, was arrested after he had slashed four works of art in the Capitol. Christy's painting received several horizontal slashes about five feet long.

(See photo on page 10.)

Hall of Columns

On the first floor beneath the House Chamber is the Hall of Columns. Stretching more than 100 feet from the south end of the House wing, the hall sports 28 columns of Massachusetts marble to hold up the hall's cast-iron ceiling. The walls are made of a gypsum compound mixed to resemble marble.

The floor of the hall was originally covered with Minton tiles like those used in the Senate wing, but the tiles were removed in the 1920's because of excessive wear. White Alabama marble and black Texas marble now cover the floor.

Statues donated by the states as part of the National Statuary Hall Collection stand among the columns lining the hall.

Corridors off the Hall of Columns lead to the Members' Dining room, meeting rooms, stairways, elevators and exits. The House Sergeant at Arms operated a small bank off one of these corridors until a 1992 scandal involving Members of Congress abusing their checking privileges forced the bank to close.

The Artwork of Allyn B. Cox

If Constantino Brumidi is the Michelangelo of the Capitol, perhaps Allyn B. Cox is its Grant Wood. While Brumidi's work echoed the masters of the Italian Renaissance, Cox painted with a truly American style.

For 31 years, from 1951 through 1982, Cox made significant contributions to the Capitol's permanent artwork. He completed Brumidi's Frieze of American History in the Rotunda—

more about this in the next chapter—and memorialized the 1969 Moon landing in the Brumidi Corridor on the first floor of the Senate wing.

From 1973 until his retirement, Cox decorated the upper walls and ceilings of corridors on the first floor of the House wing with scenes from American history. Cox's artwork shows such events as the Inaugurations of George Washington and Abraham Lincoln. Another section depicts buildings that have served as the capitol. These include Independence Hall in Philadelphia, Federal Hall in New York, and the Maryland State House in Annapolis. A panel in this section depicts the burning of the Capitol by the British in 1814.

After Cox's retirement in 1982, at age 85, the murals were completed by his associate, Cliff Young. A third artist, Jeffrey Greene, later added artwork showing the country's western expansion to the ceilings of two short cross corridors adjacent to Cox and Young's work. The Greene murals were dedicated in 1994.

The Cox Corridors were the brainchild of former Rep. Fred Schwengel of Iowa, founder and first president of the U.S. Capitol Historical Society. Schwengel felt the corridors on the first floor of the House wing needed historical artwork like that Brumidi created for the Senate corridors at the other end of the building. The historical society financed the work by Cox and his successors as a gift to the Capitol and the country.

★ ★ ★

THE NAKED TRUTH

Few, if any, of the hordes of tourists who gaze up at Allyn Cox's artwork realize that the figures on the ceiling started out as nudes. (They didn't stay that way for long.)

Cox told a Washington Post *reporter in 1982 that he would always try to make sure the clothing on the major figures in his work looked right. He said the best way he found to do this was to paint the figures in the nude at first, then add the clothes.*

★ ★ ★

ALL IN A ROW

Statues from the National Statuary Hall collection line the Hall of Columns on the first floor of the House wing.

PHOTO CREDIT:
Jeff Lesnik

FIRST CAPITOL INAUGURATION · 1829

**SWEARING IN
"OLD HICKORY"**

Andrew Jackson was the first
President sworn in on the East
Front of the Capitol. The event
is commemorated in artwork
by Allyn B. Cox on the first
floor of the House wing.

4

UNDER THE DOME

The center section of the Capitol plays a role in uniting the House and Senate, both physically and symbolically. It was also the last part of the original Capitol to be built.

The most striking room in the Capitol is located here. The Rotunda, the round room directly beneath the dome, awes visitors with its size and artwork. Below it, the Crypt provides a more intimate setting for displays about the Capitol and its history.

For nearly 100 years, the Library of Congress was housed in the western section of this part of the Capitol, but the library's former quarters have been subdivided as office space for the House and Senate, and deep in the vaults below the Crypt is an empty tomb created for George and Martha Washington.

The Rotunda

The concept of a central round room beneath the dome was the brainchild of the Capitol's first architect, William Thornton, but it was not until Charles Bulfinch took over the restoration of the building after the British attack that work began on this section of the Capitol.

The Rotunda is 96 feet in diameter and its sandstone walls stand 48 feet high. In this room, deceased Presidents, Members of Congress, Unknown Soldiers and other honored persons have lain in funerary repose.

The Rotunda was once a very lively place. Originally designed as a ceremonial space, in the early 19th Century the round hall was usually occupied by food vendors. Later it became a popular venue for fundraising receptions and society functions.

Centennial tea parties were held here in 1874 to raise money for the nation's 100th anniversary celebration. The parties were not as successful as the sponsors had hoped. Many Washingtonians felt an enthusiastic celebration of our independence from Great Britain might offend Queen Victoria.

Many of those who did attend one such party were disappointed that Hawaii's King Kalakuua, who was visiting Washington at the time, did not drop by.

Another fundraising tea, this time for Garfield Memorial Hospital, was held in the Rotunda in 1882. President Chester A. Arthur, Supreme Court Justice Samuel Miller and a number of diplomats attended the affair, which raised several thousand dollars for the hospital.

Today, the Rotunda is occasionally used for special functions. In 1985, President Ronald Reagan took the oath of office for his second term in the Rotunda when blustery weather drove the ceremony indoors. Most commonly, though, the room is filled with tourists admiring the artwork.

The Canopy

Artist Constantino Brumidi painted his masterpiece, *Apotheosis of Washington*, on the canopy 180 feet above the Rotunda floor. Working atop a high wooden scaffold, Brumidi idealized the first President, showing him ascending into a golden sky, surrounded by historical, mythological and allegorical figures. In order for the figures to be easily viewed from the floor far below, Brumidi painted them more than twice life size, some of them 15 feet (5 meters) high. The work took Brumidi 11 months to complete.

Washington is shown seated, wearing his military uniform, and flanked by female figures representing Liberty and Victory. Thirteen maidens, representing the original 13 states, complete the inner circle.

The outer circle of the fresco consists of six groupings:

Science: Minerva, Roman goddess of wisdom is shown with American inventors Benjamin Franklin, Samuel F. B. Morse and Robert Fulton.

Marine: A shell carries the chariot of Neptune, the Roman god of the sea, while the goddess Venus rises from the water holding the Transatlantic Cable, the telegraph line that linked America with Europe.

Commerce: Robert Morris, whose banking prowess helped the 13 colonies raise money to fight the Revolutionary War, is shown receiving a bag of gold from Mercury, the Roman god of Commerce.

Mechanics: Vulcan, Roman god of fire, stands before a forge with his foot atop a cannon barrel and newly made cannon balls stacked nearby.

Agriculture: The Roman goddess Ceres, the goddess of agriculture and fertility, rides a horse-drawn reaper while a young man, representing the young American nation, holds the reins.

War: A female figure of Armed Freedom, with cape, sword and shield and accompanied by an American bald eagle with arrows in its claws, is shown vanquishing tyranny and royal authority.

★ ★ ★

GEORGE'S GIRLS

When Brumidi created the Apotheosis, *he needed models for the arch of young maidens representing the 13 original colonies.*

Frank G. Carpenter, Washington correspondent for the Cleveland Leader *in the 1880's, wrote in one of his columns, "(Brumidi) is said to have been a free liver, and the story is told that the thirteen fair faces which look down into the Rotunda include those of certain ladies of questionable reputation with whom he was acquainted."*

In other words, Brumidi's work may show the Father of Our Country surrounded by ladies of the evening.

George doesn't seem to mind.

★ ★ ★

History on the Walls

The walls of the Rotunda are decorated with eight huge (12 feet by 18 feet) oil paintings depicting the arrival of European explorers and colonists in North America and the founding of the independent United States.

Four of them, on the west walls of the Rotunda, were commissioned in 1817 and were painted by John Trumbull, who had briefly served as an aide to George Washington during the Revolutionary War. Trumbull painted most of the people depicted in his paintings from life. That is, he painted them in person, as opposed to drawing them from memory or using another work of art as a model. (There was no photography at the time.)

The four Trumbull paintings depict important events of the Revolution and the nation's founding:

The Declaration of Independence in Congress, at the Independence Hall, Philadelphia, July 4th, 1776—In Philadelphia in July of 1776, representatives of the 13 American colonies declared their independence from the King of England. The

Declaration, drafted by Thomas Jefferson, declared that "all men are created equal" and have "unalienable rights," including "life, liberty and the pursuit of happiness." The colonists further declared that all governments derive "their just powers from the consent of the governed," and that, when the government becomes repressive, "it is the right of the people to alter or abolish it." After listing a lengthy series of offenses the crown had committed against the colonies, the assembly declared the colonies to be "free and independent states; that they are absolved from all allegiances to the British Crown, and that all political connection between them and the State of Great Britain is and ought to be totally dissolved." In support of their declaration, the signers pledged "our lives, our fortunes, and our sacred honor."

The Trumbull painting shows 42 of the 56 men who signed the Declaration, including Benjamin Franklin, future Presidents Jefferson and John Adams, and John Hancock, president of the Congress, whose famous, large signature is the most recognizable on the document.

An engraving of this painting adorns the back of the $2 bill. (Yes, there actually is a $2 bill!)

The Surrender of General Burgoyne at Saratoga, New York, October 17th, 1777—The Battle of Saratoga, fought in upstate New York in the fall of 1777, was a turning point in the Revolution. European powers were reluctant to recognize the young nation's independence until they were certain that the Americans could stand up to the British Army. The British, at the same time, thought they could bring a quick end to the war by controlling the Hudson River Valley and separating New England from the rest of the colonies. When Americans commanded by Gen. Horatio Gates defeated British forces led by Gen. John Burgoyne at Saratoga, the colonies remained united and the Americans had their decisive victory. Soon after, France joined the war on the side of the Americans.

The painting shows Gen. Burgoyne, in his red British uniform coat, offering his sword to Gen. Gates, at the center of the scene, wearing colonial blue. Although Gates accepted the surrender, he allowed the Redcoat to keep his sword.

Surrender of Lord Cornwallis at Yorktown, Virginia, October 19, 1781—The Battle of Yorktown, Virginia, in 1781 was the final victory for the Americans. Penned in by ground troops commanded by Gen. Washington and the French fleet offshore, the British commander, Lord Cornwallis, was forced to surrender. Gen. Cornwallis refused to admit he had been bested by colonials, and had subordinate officers deliver his message. The painting shows American General Benjamin Lincoln, on a white horse at the center, riding between lines of American and French troops. General Washington is on the right, astride a brown horse.

General George Washington Resigning His Commission to Congress as Commander in Chief of the Army.—In December, 1783, at the end of the Revolutionary War, George Washington made the decision to leave military service and return to his private life as a gentleman farmer. Washington was a national hero and commanded the loyalty of the Continental Army. At the same time, the young nation was struggling with the formation of a system of government to carry it into its future. Washington could have been king. He could have established a military dictatorship. Instead, he chose to be a citizen.

The Trumbull painting shows Washington, dressed in his military uniform, addressing Congress. Looking on are future Presidents Thomas Jefferson, James Madison and James Monroe. Martha Washington is also in the picture, although she did not attend the actual event, which took place at the State House in Annapolis, Maryland.

VICTORY AT YORKTOWN

John Trumbull's painting *Surrender of Lord Cornwallis at Yorktown, Virginia, October 19th, 1781* depicts the American colonists' final victory over the British army.

PHOTO CREDIT:
Architect of the Capitol
Neg. no. 70223

On the east walls of the Rotunda are four scenes from the exploration and early colonial periods of American history by four different artists:

Discovery of the Mississippi by De Soto, A.D. 1541 (William Powell, 1855)—In 1539, the Spanish explorer Hernando De Soto landed on the west coast of Florida, near the mouth of Tampa Bay. De Soto and his men explored the Gulf Coast and the swampy forests of the Deep South. In 1541, the expedition reached the Mississippi River, becoming the first Europeans to see the great river.

Powell's painting shows De Soto, wearing a plumed hat, mounted on a horse and greeted by a Native American chief, who offers the Spaniard a peace pipe.

Powell's work romanticizes De Soto's expedition. In reality, the explorer's relations with the native peoples were not as peaceful as the painting depicts. De Soto, a disciple of the Conquistador Francisco Pizarro, was in search of golden treasures such as those found among the Incas of Peru. He made war with most of the local tribes he encountered and imprisoned many of their number. He burned settlements and captured grain and livestock. By the time the expedition reached the banks of the Mississippi, De Soto and his men were ragged, hungry, sick and wounded from years of fighting their way through the wilderness. De Soto himself died a year later and his men, fearful that the local tribes would discover and desecrate his grave, sank De Soto's body in the Mississippi. The remainder of the expedition worked its way south and eventually reached Spanish settlements in Mexico.

Landing of Columbus at the Island of Guanahani, West Indies, October 12th, 1492 (John Vanderlyn, 1847)—Christopher Columbus is credited with discovering America. Of course, when he arrived he was greeted by Native Americans who had been around for centuries. Even among the Europeans,

A JOURNEY OF DISCOVERY

The painting *Discovery of the Mississippi by De Soto A.D. 1541* by William H. Powell romanticizes the Spanish explorer's journey through what is now the southeastern United States.

PHOTO CREDIT:
Architect of the Capitol
Neg. no. 70223

there is evidence that the Vikings and even Irish sailors may have gotten here first. Still, Columbus' voyages on behalf of the Spanish crown began the European colonization of the Americas that eventually led to, among other things, the founding of the United States of America.

Vanderlyn shows Columbus landing in the West Indies on October 12, 1492. He plants the flag of Spain to claim the land for King Ferdinand and Queen Isabella, while curious native people watch from the trees.

Embarkation of the Pilgrims at Delft Haven, Holland, July 22nd, 1620 (Robert W. Weir, 1844)—In the summer of 1620, four months before landing at Plymouth Rock, the Puritan dissidents we know as the Pilgrims began their journey in Holland.

The painting shows a group of the religious refugees, including Miles Standish and William Bradford, praying on the deck of the ship *Speedwell* before leaving Delft Haven, Holland, on a journey that will eventually bring them to Massachusetts. The *Speedwell* wasn't seaworthy enough to make the second part of the journey, from Plymouth, England, to the New World. Its passengers had to be carried across the ocean by the *Speedwell's* sister ship, the *Mayflower*.

Baptism of Pocahontas at Jamestown, Virginia, 1613 (John Gadsby Chapman, 1840)—Pocahontas was the daughter of Chief Powhattan at the time the first permanent English settlement in North America was taking root at Jamestown, Virginia. Although popular history links her name with Englishman John Smith, Pocahontas married another colonist, John Rolfe. In preparation for her marriage, the first between a Native American and an English colonist, Pocahontas accepted the Christian faith and adopted the Christian name Rebecca.

In the painting, Pocahontas is shown dressed in white, kneeling before the Anglican minister. Looking on are Rolfe and other colonists, as well as Chief Powhattan and other members of Pocahontas' family.

BEST FOOT FORWARD

One of the figures in the painting, The Baptism of Pocahontas, *is Opechancanough, brother of Chief Powhattan and uncle to Pocahontas. He is seated on the floor, facing forward, giving the viewer a good look at his six-toed left foot.*

Historians know Opechancanough as the tribal leader who tried to wipe out Jamestown colony in 1622 and again in 1644. Legions of tourists know him as the six-toed Indian in the Capitol.

More History on the Walls

American history is also displayed in carvings high on the Rotunda walls.

Four relief sculptures adorn the walls above each of the room's four entrances. They are *The Landing of the Pilgrims* by Enrico Causici, *The Conflict of Daniel Boone and the Indians,* also by Causici, *The Preservation of John Smith by Pocahontas* by Antonio Capanello, and *William Penn's Treaty with the Indians,* by Nicholas Gevelot.

In addition, four Europeans who played significant parts in the exploration of America are honored in wreathed panels carved in the walls above the historic paintings. The four are Christopher Columbus, who began the age of European settlement in the Americas; John Cabot, who explored the North Atlantic coast for England; Sir Walter Raleigh, who established the first English colony in America on Roanoke Island, along the coast of what is now North Carolina; and Robert Cavalier, sieur de La Salle, who explored the Mississippi Valley from the Great Lakes to the Gulf of Mexico and claimed the region, which he named Louisiana, for France.

CIRCLE OF HISTORY

The Frieze of American History circles the interior of the dome above the Rotunda.

PHOTO CREDIT:
Jeff Lesnik

55

The Frieze of American History

Around the midsection of the dome above the Rotunda is a "belt" in tones of brown and white depicting significant events in American history. Begun by Brumidi in 1878, the *Frieze of American History* uses monochromatic pigments and the fresco technique to create a continuous series of flat images that appear to be three-dimensional.

Brumidi designed the frieze and completed the first one-third of the work himself before a serious accident shortened his career, and likely his life. In late 1879, while working on the frieze from a scaffolding high above the floor, Brumidi's chair slipped and the artist began to fall from the structure. The 74-year-old Brumidi saved himself by grabbing the rung of a ladder and hung there for some 15 minutes until rescuers helped him down. Although Brumidi returned to work, he spent little time on the scaffold, choosing instead to work on his sketches for the frieze figures. The artist died a few months later.

Artist Filippo Costaggini was hired to complete the frieze, but when he was finished in 1889, Costaggini discovered that Brumidi had miscalculated. His design ended 31 feet short.

Costaggini added three of his own panels to fill some of the space, but the remaining 15 feet remained blank until 1951 when Allyn B. Cox was commissioned to finish the job.

The three artists' combined work shows the progression of American history from the landing of Columbus to the flight of the Wright Brothers.

Even though there's no more room, the completion of the frieze did not mean the end of history. Dedicating the work in 1954, President Dwight D. Eisenhower said, "The thought does not cross the mind that the history of America has been completed. The statue atop the Capitol faces east, toward the rising sun of each new day."

Bulfinch's Library

The Library of Congress resided in the Capitol for nearly 100 years. For most of that time the library occupied the west-central section of the building. Architect Charles Bulfinch designed a beautiful space with a comfortable, ornate reading room where visitors could look out over the Capitol's west lawn.

(above)
A PEACEFUL PLACE

The Capitol's Prayer Room provides Senators and Representatives with a place for quiet contemplation.

PHOTO CREDIT:
Library of Congress
Neg. no. LC-USA7-11729

THE OLD LIBRARY

The Library of Congress occupied the west-central section of the Capitol from 1824 until it moved to the Jefferson Building across from the Capitol grounds in 1897.

PHOTO CREDIT:
Library of Congress
Neg. no. LC-USZ62-601

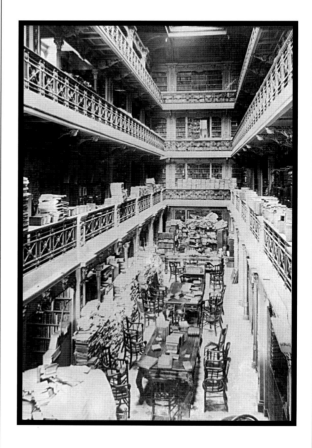

In 1851, fire tore through the library, destroying many of the books and works of art in the library's collection. Thomas U. Walter rebuilt the rooms in fireproof cast-iron.

When the Library of Congress moved to its own building at the end of the century, the ironwork was dismantled and sold, and the space was subdivided into offices and meeting rooms.

The Prayer Room

Just off the Rotunda is a small room where Members can meditate and pray in solitude. The Prayer Room is open whenever the House or Senate is in session. The nondenominational facility, opened in 1955, features a stained glass window showing George Washington kneeling, with his head bent and hands folded in prayer.

The Crypt

Directly below the Rotunda is the Crypt. The room's primary job is to support the floor of the Rotunda above it. It does this with forty stout, sandstone columns arranged in concentric rings and supporting the room's vaulted ceiling.

The Crypt was originally open to the Rotunda above through a hole in the Rotunda's floor in order to bring light down into the lower chamber, but cold air and dampness from the Crypt made it difficult to heat the Rotunda and Bulfinch decided to close up the floor.

Today the Crypt is used as a display area for photographs and artifacts explaining the architecture and artwork of the Capitol.

I'VE GOT A SECRET

A nondescript elevator fronted by a sign reading "Authorized Personnel Only" leads from the Crypt to the Capitol's fourth floor. That's where the nation's secrets are kept.

Secure rooms operated by the House Select Committee on Intelligence and the Secretary of the Senate contain sensitive government documents for inspection by Members of Congress and select staff.

Only Members and those staff who have appropriate security clearances may enter these rooms.

Plans call for these rooms to be replaced by new, updated secure facilities in the new Capitol Visitors Center, expected to be completed in 2005.

East Central Hall

Just off the Crypt is East Central Hall. The area was created by the East Front extension project of 1958-62. The hall contains visitor services, including a bookshop, post office, restrooms and even an Amtrak ticket office.

Statues in East Central Hall are restricted to those contributed by the 13 original states.

A unique meeting room, EF-100, is adjacent to this hall. The room, located under the center steps of the East Front, is often used as a holding room for VIP's who visit the Capitol. The room's rough stone walls belie the fact that it was not part of the original building but a much later addition. EF-100 is unique for another reason. Since it is equidistant from the House and Senate, its room number does not bear the H (for House) or S (for Senate) designation given most other spaces in the Capitol.

EF-100 is scheduled to be removed as part of the Capitol Visitors Center project.

George Washington's Tomb

Beneath the floor of the Crypt lies George and Martha Washington's tomb—only without George and Martha.

When George Washington died in 1799, a three-way tug-of-war began over where his body should be buried. Washington's last will and testament stated that he wished to be buried on the grounds of his estate at Mount Vernon, Virginia. That didn't stop politicians in Washington, D.C., or Richmond, Virginia, from trying to lay claim to Washington's remains.

Shortly after his death, Congress passed a resolution calling for the construction of a mausoleum inside the Capitol, but no further action was taken. A year later, a second resolution called for building a mausoleum on the Capitol grounds. Architect B. Henry Latrobe designed a pyramid 100 feet square at the base with Greek Revival ornamentation, but no funds were appropriated for the project, so the mausoleum was never built.

In 1816, the Virginia legislature voted to move Washington's body to Richmond. This prompted another move in Congress to bring the remains to the Capitol. A tomb was readied in the vaults below the Crypt. After much negotiation, though, Washington's heirs decided that he should not be buried in either Washington or Richmond, but his remains should remain at Mount Vernon.

THE EMPTY TOMB

A tomb for George and Martha Washington was built into the lower vaults of the Capitol, but negotiations with the Washingtons' heirs failed to dislodge the couple's remains from Mt. Vernon.

PHOTO CREDIT:
Library of Congress
Neg. no. LC-USA7-27168

Today the tomb in the Capitol stands empty except for the Lincoln Catafalque, a wooden bier draped in black velvet, originally used to hold the casket of President Abraham Lincoln when the assassinated President lay in state at the Capitol in 1865. The catafalque has been used whenever the body of a high ranking offical has lain in state in the Capitol since then.

Vaults, Terraces and Courtyards

Vaults in the lower levels of the Capitol have served many purposes over the building's first two centuries. In the 19th Century, books from the Library of Congress, and the records of the House, Senate and Supreme Court were stored here. During the Civil War, the lower committee rooms of the Capitol were converted to bakeries to help feed the Union Army.

When the Library and Court moved to their own buildings in 1897 and 1935, much of the storage area in the lower levels of the Capitol was converted to office space. Removal of Congressional records to the National Archives in the early 20th Century freed additional space.

The addition of terraces to the West Front in the 1800's created many rooms now used for offices and meeting rooms. These rooms are numbered with the designation HT (House Terrace) or ST (Senate Terrace). A 1993-94 project to fill in lower courtyards on the West Front created more meeting space. These rooms carry the designation HC or SC (for House or Senate Courtyard).

CAPITOL HONORS

The remains of the Unknown
Soldiers of World War II and the
Korean Conflict lie in honor in the
Rotunda in 1958 en route to their
final resting place at Arlington
National Cemetary.

5
ON THE OUTSIDE

The exterior view of the Capitol is one of the most recognizable facades in the world. The back of the U.S. $50 bill is just one of the many places where the Capitol and its dome are immortalized. State capitols throughout the country have copied its architectural formula of two wings topped by a dome.

The Dome

The most distinguishing feature of the Capitol is the magnificent cast-iron dome. Designed by Thomas U. Walter in 1854, the new structure replaced the original dome built by Charles Bulfinch thirty years earlier.

The inclusion of a dome in the Capitol's design was due in large part to the influence of George Washington, who thought a dome would add a touch of grandeur to the building. William Thornton's original design for the Capitol featured a low dome over a central rotunda. When Bulfinch built the center section of the building in the 1820's, he included a higher "tortoise shell" dome of wood and copper.

Bulfinch's dome, though fine for its time, needed constant repair and posed a fire hazard. Once the new House and Senate wings were added in the 1850's, the Bulfinch dome was out of proportion with the enlarged building.

Walter saw the need for a new crown for the Capitol. He drew his inspiration from the classical domes of Europe: St. Peter's Basilica in Rome, St. Paul's Cathedral in London, the Panthèon in Paris and St. Isaac's Cathedral in St. Petersburg, Russia. According to a diary kept by August Gottlieb Schoenborn, principal draftsman at the Capitol and confidant of Walter, St. Isaac's provided the principal inspiration. Schoenborn wrote that Walter's design was identical to the dome of St. Isaac's in some of its measurements and similar in several others.

Walter illustrated his ideas for a new dome in a drawing, which he then hung in his Capitol office.

The design so charmed Members of Congress that the House and Senate speedily came up with $100,000 to begin work on the new dome.

Work began in 1856. Bulfinch's dome was removed and replaced with a temporary roof to protect the Rotunda and its artwork. A scaffold was built through the center of the temporary roof to hold a construction boom for hauling up the materials for the new dome.

Despite the fast start, work on the new dome had its complications. Walter had several disagreements with Capt. Montgomery C. Meigs, who supervised construction for the Army Corps of Engineers. Walter complained that Meigs would make changes in the dome's design without consulting the architect, so Walter withheld his drawings. Meigs retaliated by refusing to pay Walter's draftsmen.

Another challenge faced Walter when sculptor Thomas Crawford designed a statue for the top of the dome that was three feet taller than Walter's original concept. This required Walter to lower the height of the dome in order to provide a wider base for the statue and maintain the overall scale of the structure.

★ ★ ★

7¢ A POUND

In 1859, the foundry of Janes, Fowler, Kirkland and Company in New York approached Capt. William Franklin, Meigs' replacement as supervising engineer, with an offer he could not refuse.

The foundry offered to complete the work on the cast-iron dome for seven cents a pound, "complete and put up." Franklin jumped on the offer and the company was hired to complete the project. The use of a single, private contractor allowed work to continue despite the outbreak of the Civil War.

★ ★ ★

The Sound of the Hammer Never Stopped

When the Civil War began in 1861, there was strong sentiment in Congress that work on the Capitol should stop until the war was over. The Corps of Engineers halted construction on the north and south wings, but work on the dome continued. Even though the contractors would not be paid for a year, they kept a small workforce at the Capitol to keep the dome project going. The company determined that the only way to protect its investment in the iron and other materials it had delivered to the Capitol grounds and keep the contract in force was to continue working. So the dome continued to rise slowly over the Capitol. President Abraham Lincoln later remarked that he saw the rising Capitol dome as a symbol of the survival of the Union with Washington as its capital. Architect Walter wrote in his report to Congress that the sound of the hammer never stopped during the national crisis.

The outer dome was completed with the installation of the Statue of Freedom in 1863. Three years later, removal of the scaffolding in the Rotunda revealed Brumidi's masterpiece *Apotheosis of Washington* on the canopy, and signaled the completion of the inner dome.

The completed dome weighs 8,909,200 pounds or nearly 4,500 tons (4,041,213 kilograms). Final cost: $1,047,291.

Today the dome is floodlit at night and can be seen for miles around. When Congress is in session after dark, a light shines in the *tholos*, the pillared tower that crowns the dome and supports the Statue of Freedom.

A set of stairs inside the dome leads to two observation decks, one about midway up the dome, the other just below the tholos. Once open to the public, access to the stairs and the observation areas is now restricted.

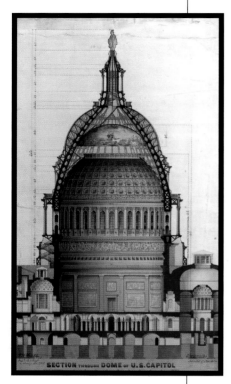

INSIDE & OUT *(above)*

Architect Walter's cutaway drawing shows the relationship between the inner and outer domes.

PHOTO CREDIT:
Library of Congress
Neg. no. 74001

FREEDOM ON HIGH

Thomas Crawford's bronze statue of Freedom tops the Capitol dome.

PHOTO CREDIT:
Library of Congress
Neg. no. LC-USA7-27-751

★ ★ ★

FOLLOWING THE SUN

The heat of the sun causes the cast-iron dome to expand by as much as three inches. As the sun moves across the sky, the swelling follows its path. At night, the dome cools and returns to its original shape.

The daily cycle of expansion and contraction over the years has caused cracks in the iron structure that require periodic repairs.

★ ★ ★

Freedom Triumphant

Just who is that lady standing more than 280 feet (83 meters) above the pavement atop the dome of the Capitol?

She is Freedom—officially *Freedom Triumphant in War and Peace*—a creation of sculptor Thomas Crawford. She is an allegorical figure, which means the statue does not depict a particular person, but uses a human form to represent an abstract concept or ideal.

Freedom stands 19.5 feet (6 meters) tall and weighs 7.5 tons (6,800 kilograms). She holds a sheathed sword in her right hand and a shield and laurel crown in her left.

Her headdress is an eagle head and feathers surrounded by stars, but it was originally designed as a soft "liberty cap," a head covering worn by freed slaves during Roman times, and a popular symbol of freedom during the French Revolution.

The liberty cap did not sit well with many Southerners, since the slavery question was still very contentious in Congress when the work was underway in the 1850's. The primary objector was Jefferson Davis, who, as Secretary of War, was in charge of the Capitol's expansion. Davis, of Mississippi, later served as President of the Confederate States during the Civil War.

As a compromise, Crawford gave Freedom a feathered headdress inspired by Native American designs, and leading some observers to mistake her for Pocahontas.

In 1993, visitors to the Capitol got a close-up view of Freedom for the first time in 130 years. In order to refurbish the statue, the Architect of the Capitol had it lifted from the Dome by helicopter and lowered onto the East Plaza. Freedom remained grounded for nearly six months as workers carefully removed dirt and corrosion, made necessary repairs and gave her a new patina of deep green.

When work was completed, Freedom was airlifted back to her perch above the Capitol.

A Tale of Two Fronts

Most buildings have a front and a back. The Capitol is one of those rare structures to have two fronts, known as the East Front and the West Front.

The East Front faces the Supreme Court and Library of Congress as well as the residential area of Capitol Hill. It has three large sets of steps, one serving the House wing, one serving the Senate wing and the a third at the center of the building leading up to the Rotunda. The steps rise from the East Plaza to the second floor of the Capitol.

From the outside, the East Front of the Capitol looks much the same as it did when Thomas U. Walter added the new House and Senate wings and the larger dome in the mid-1800's. One major change that is not always apparent is the East Front extension, done under the supervision of Architect of the Capitol J. George Stewart in 1958-62. When the east facade of the original Capitol building and the two connecting corridors to the House and Senate extensions were covered over with the new addition, the old sandstone facades were painstakingly copied in marble.

EXPANDING THE CAPITOL

The Capitol's center steps and portico are removed as workers prepare to extend the East Front in 1959.

PHOTO CREDIT:
Library of Congress
Neg. no. LC-USA7-14732

So exact was the copy that casual observers are hard-pressed to discern old photographs of the building from more recent photos. (Hint: Look for the flagpole in front of the dome. If the pole is up close to the dome, the photograph is pre-1958. If there is a discernable distance between the dome and the flagpole, it is a more recent shot.)

The East Front was the traditional site of Presidential inaugurations from Andrew Jackson to Jimmy Carter. In 1981, with President Ronald Reagan's first inaugural, the ceremony moved to the West Front because the West Lawn offered more area for public seating and unobstructed views.

THE EAST FRONT

The Capitol's East Front and East Plaza, with the House wing in the foreground.

PHOTO CREDIT:
Jeff Lesnik

★ ★ ★

FOR THE BIRDS

The nooks and crannies around the dome and stonework of the Capitol made dandy nesting places for pigeons and starlings, a fact not lost on the pesky birds.

In order to protect the building from the damage these birds could do, not to mention the mess they can make, in 1962 the Capitol was outfitted with an electrified system to keep the birds away. The system consists of a network of charged wires that give a mild and unwelcome shock to any bird touching them.

A similar bird deterrent system was installed at the Supreme Court building across the street.

★ ★ ★

Porticos and Pediments

The East Front of the Capitol features three sets of steps, each leading to a *portico*, a pillared shelter or porch. Above each portico is a triangular *pediment* containing a sculpture.

Peace Protecting Genius, a work by Luigi Perisco from a design suggested by John Quincy Adams, was installed in the pediment above the East Center portico in 1828. The original Perisco sculpture graced the pediment for more than 130 years. The sandstone work, badly deteriorated over the years, was replaced by a facsimile in marble by sculptor Bruno Mankowski during the East Front extension project in 1960.

The work depicts female figures representing America, Justice and Hope. The central figure, America, holds a shield bearing the letters "USA." The shield rests on an altar inscribed with the date, "July 4, 1776," the date most closely associated with the Declaration of Independence. An eagle is perched at her feet. The figure of Justice holds scales in one hand and a parchment scroll bearing the date September 17, 1787, the date of the signing of the Constitution, in the other. The arm of the figure of Hope rests on an anchor, a classical symbol of hope.

When the new House and Senate wings were added to the building in the 1850's, a portico was included on the East Front of each of the new additions. The Senate (north) portico displays in its pediment *Progress of Civilization,* by Thomas Crawford, the same sculptor who created the Statue of Freedom. The work, completed in 1854, depicts the settlement of the North American continent with figures representing European and Native American cultures flanking a female representation of America.

The pediment above the House (south) portico stood empty for 43 years before the sculpture *Apotheosis of Democracy,* by Paul Wayland Bartlett was installed in 1916. The central figures of the work show Peace protecting Genius. They are flanked by figures representing Agriculture and Industry.

Columbus Doors

Standing at the central entrance at the East Front of the Capitol are the massive bronze doors known as the Columbus Doors. Designed as the entrance to the new House wing from Statuary Hall, the doors were installed in 1863. They attracted so much attention that visitors examining them often blocked the entrance. Complaining Members finally had the doors moved to the east-central entrance in 1871. They were removed and preserved during the East Front extension project, and reinstalled in their present location.

The doors stand almost 17 feet high and weigh nearly 10 tons. They feature nine relief panels depicting important events in the life of Christopher Columbus. The lunette at the top of the doors shows Columbus arriving in the New World. A bust of the explorer tops the frame.

The West Front

The West Front faces the National Mall, the Smithsonian Museums, the White House and the commercial district of Washington. The central section of the West Front is the only facade of the original Capitol building still exposed to the outside.

As the building aged, the structural integrity of the West Front drew more and more concern. By the mid-20th Century, heavy beams were installed on the exterior to brace the wall. In 1955, plans were made to extend the East and West Fronts, to improve structural stability and add office space. Architectural purists and historical preservationists opposed the work. A decision was made to extend only the East Front.

HONORING COLUMBUS

The life and explorations of Christopher Columbus are preserved in the bronze doors that lead from the East Plaza into the Rotunda.

PHOTO CREDIT:
Architect of the Capitol
Neg. no. 70769

The question of repairs to the West Front were left unanswered until 1983, when Congress authorized $49 million to restore the facade.

By the time the work was completed four years later, 40 coats of paint were removed from the exterior wall, 40 percent of the sandstone blocks were replaced, and 1,000 steel rods were inserted in the wall to reinforce it.

The work was done at night so as not to disturb Congress in session during the day. Under the supervision of Architect of the Capitol George White, the project was completed in 1987, ahead of schedule and under budget.

The West Front features distinctive terraces and two stairways leading down to a broad lawn. Bulfinch added the first terraces as storage areas for coal and firewood. Olmsted replaced these with even grander terraces of marble to create a "pedestal" for the Capitol. The terraces also provide access to the building from the West Lawn and a pleasing vantage point for viewing the monuments and museums along the Mall.

The West Front sports three flagpoles. The center pole in front of the Dome flies the U.S. flag 24 hours a day, a tradition dating back to World War I.

Poles above the House and Senate wings only display the flag when that particular chamber is in session.

★ ★ ★

SPIN CONTROL

In 1960, the Architect of the Capitol began to get complaints about the speed of the revolving door at the West Front entrance to the Capitol.

The door spun so easily that most users pushed it too fast for some of the slower folks who found themselves caught in its revolutions. The speed of the door was especially a problem for older people and small children. Some injuries even resulted from the speedy rotation.

To fix the problem, the Architect requested $4,000 for a speed-control device to keep the door turning at the safe pace of 12 revolutions per minute.

It marked one of the few times when people complained that something in Washington was moving too fast.

★ ★ ★

NEW DIGS

The Capitol Visitors Center, the newest addition to the building, is under construction at the Capitol's East Front. The underground facility is scheduled to open 2005.

PHOTO CREDIT:
Jim Berard

FLAG SIGNALS

The West Front of the Capitol features three flagpoles: one in front of the dome and one each over the House and Senate wings. The center flag flies 24 hours a day. The other two fly when that chamber is meeting. In this photo, the flag at the left is over the Senate wing, showing that the Senate is in session. The flagpole on the right is empty, indicating that the House was not meeting when the photo was taken.

PHOTO CREDIT:

Jim Berard

6

CONGRESS: THE ORDINARY AND THE EXTRAORDINARY

Our system of government relies on a steady stream of dedicated individuals who are willing to take on the often messy business of making our nation's laws. Former Speaker Jim Wright called them "ordinary people doing extraordinary things."

This chapter is dedicated to those people and events, the ordinary and the extraordinary, that are a part of the history of the U.S. Capitol.

Senate Youngsters

One of the greatest men to serve in the U.S. Senate assumed his seat in violation of the U.S. Constitution. And he wasn't the only one to do it.

The Constitution sets three requirements for membership in the U.S. Senate. A Senator must be a citizen of the United States for at least nine years, must reside in the state from which he or she is elected, and must be at least 30 years of age. In the Senate's early years, at least three new arrivals snuck into the body under the legal age limit.

In 1806, Kentucky sent a young Henry Clay to the Senate to serve out an unexpired term of an expired Senator. The Senators of the day conveniently overlooked the Constitutionally required minimum age of 30 and welcomed the 29-year-old Clay to their ranks.

In 1816, 28-year-old Armistead Mason of Virginia was allowed to take a seat in the Senate. Mason died in a duel three years later.

Another youngster, John H. Eaton of Tennessee, was allowed to take his seat in 1818. At 28 years, three months, Eaton holds the distinction of being the youngest person ever to have served —legally or otherwise— in the U.S. Senate.

Congressional Lizardry

When Congressional District lines are drawn to favor a particular party or candidate, they are said to have been "gerrymandered." The name comes from Elbridge Gerry, a signer of the Declaration of Independence, a delegate to the Constitutional Convention, a Representative from Massachusetts in the First and Second Congresses (1793-1794) and Vice President under James Madison (1813-1814).

As Governor of Massachusetts in 1812, Gerry (pronounced with a hard "g" like "Gary") had state legislative districts drawn in a way that favored his political allies. One district was of such an odd, elongated shape that an observer likened it to a lizard or a salamander. A companion, noting the Governor's hand in drawing the district, quipped that it wasn't a salamander, but a "Gerry-mander."

Since then, the word *gerrymander* (now with a soft "g" to sound like "Jerry") has applied to similar attempts to draw legislative or Congressional districts to further political goals.

Genius and Infamy

Aaron Burr could have been one of our nation's greatest figures. In fact, Burr could have been the third President of the United States, instead of Thomas Jefferson. In the election of 1800, Burr and Jefferson found themselves with the same number of electoral votes. The election was thrown into the House of Representatives, and, after 36 ballots, Jefferson was declared the winner. As the runner-up, Burr was handed the consolation prize: the office of Vice President.[2]

Burr is best known for the duel in which he took the life of Alexander Hamilton. Hamilton and Burr were long-time rivals. As attorneys in New York, they often faced each other in court. As

2 Under the original provisions of the Constitution, the candidate receiving the most electoral votes was elected President; the person who received the second-highest total was elected Vice President. In the 1800 election, the House of Representatives broke the tie and declared Jefferson the winner and Burr the runner-up. The 12th Amendment, ratified in 1804, changed the process so that electors voted separately for President and Vice President. In modern practice, the President and Vice-President are elected as a team.

(opposite page)

GIANTS IN THE SENATE

Henry Clay addresses the Senate as John C. Calhoun and others look on in the engraving *U.S. Senate, A.D. 1850* by Peter F. Rothermel

PHOTO CREDIT:
U.S. Senate Collection
Neg. no. 38.00029.000

politicians, they were polar opposites. Hamilton was a Federalist and supported a strong central government; Burr was a Democratic-Republican, and favored decentralized government with most of the power in the hands of the states.

Still, the two men maintained a professional, courteous, even friendly relationship, until Hamilton tried to discredit Burr during and after the 1800 Presidential election. When Hamilton's criticism cost Burr a shot at the governorship of New York, Burr thought the time had come to take a shot at Hamilton.

The two fought a duel at Weehauken, New Jersey on the morning of July 11, 1804. Burr was charged with murder in Hamilton's death, but was never convicted. He resumed his duties as Vice President and finished out his term.

In 1807, the so-called Burr Conspiracy was uncovered. Burr and associates had planned to seize land in the Southwest, either in the new Louisiana Territory or in lands then held by Spain, and create a new country with Burr as its head. He was tried for treason in August of 1807, but was acquitted.

After four years in Europe, Burr returned to New York City where he practiced law until 1812.

Burr was only 13 when he entered the College of New Jersey (now Princeton University). He graduated at 16. At age 20, he was given the rank of captain in the Continental Army. Burr's youth held a world of promise.

Woodrow Wilson, a fellow Princetonian, put it best when he said Burr had "genius enough to have made him immortal, and unschooled passion enough to have made him infamous."

Going to the Dogs

John Randolph of Roanoke, who served as a Representative and later a Senator from Virginia, was one of the more colorful characters of the early days of Congress. Tall, thin and eloquent, Randolph presented a striking figure on the floor and was a formidable adversary for anyone who dared engage in debate with him.

Determinedly independent, Randolph refused to be labeled either a Federalist or a Democratic-Republican, the two political divisions of the day. Instead, Randolph called himself *tertium quid*, Latin for "a third thing."

While serving in the House, Randolph routinely brought his hunting dog with him into the chamber, and even struck a fellow Congressman with his cane for complaining about the noise the dog made. When Henry Clay was elected Speaker in 1815, he wouldn't put up with Randolph's eccentric ways and banished the dog from the House Chamber.

Today, many Members of Congress are still very attached to their pets and often bring them to work with them. Although they don't bring their dogs onto the floor of the House or Senate, as Randolph did, Sen. Edward Kennedy of Massachusetts once brought his Portuguese water dog, Splash, to a conference committee meeting, and let Splash hop up into the chairman's seat.

Stop the Presses

The First Amendment to the Constitution guarantees freedom of the press, but the ink was barely dry on the Bill of Rights when Congress enacted the Alien and Sedition Act of 1798. At the time the Act was passed, there was great fear that America was on an unavoidable path to war with the revolutionary government of France. The Act prohibited the publication of any false or malicious statement against the Federalist-controlled Congress or President John Adams. It was a deliberate attempt to silence papers sympathetic to Thomas Jefferson and his Democratic-Republican Party.

William Duane, editor of a pro-Jefferson, anti-Federalist Philadelphia newspaper, *The Aurora*, ran afoul of the Act. He published a Federalist-sponsored bill that called for the appointment of a special commission to review votes in the up-coming Presidential election of 1800 and decide which electoral votes should be counted. (The Supreme Court played much the same role in the Presidential election of 2000, but that's another story for another book.)

Duane's story outraged Jefferson's supporters who saw the commission as an unconstitutional device to ensure Adams' reelection. Unfortunately, Duane mistakenly wrote that the bill had passed the Senate, when it had not. The Federalist Senators had their cause of action against Duane: He had printed something false about Congress. The editor was hauled before the Senate, but managed to avoid any serious punishment by hiding out until Jefferson and his supporters were in power.

Reporter William Nugent of *The New York Herald* did not escape the Senate's wrath in 1848 when he reported on the secret treaty that ended the Mexican War. Nugent was arrested by the Sergeant at Arms. When he refused to disclose his sources, Nugent was ordered imprisoned in a committee hearing room. While so incarcerated, Nugent continued to draw his salary and issued daily dispatches under the dateline "Custody of the Sergeant at Arms."

After a month, the Senate gave up and let Nugent go.

More recently, the Senate unleashed its collective rage against *Roll Call*, a newspaper that covers the behind-the-scenes activities of Congress. In 1957, the paper was banned from the Senate news-stands and would no longer be delivered through the Senate mail.

Roll Call had run an article and an editorial on the way officers were appointed to the Capitol Police force. The editorial asked questions about the process, but took no position. Nonetheless,

the Senate Sergeant at Arms, whose office over-sees the police force, ordered the ban on the news-paper.

Sergeant at Arms Joseph C. Duke insisted the ban had nothing to do with the content of the paper, but with the burden delivery placed on the mail system.

The action did not affect the paper's circulation on the House side of the Capitol.

The King of the Wild Frontier

Famed in legend and song, Rep. Davy Crockett of Tennessee may or may not have "killed him a bear when he was only three." He did command a bat-talion of riflemen under General Andrew Jackson during the War of 1812, and served a total of three terms in the U.S. House of Representatives, 1827-1831 and 1833-34.

Not a particularly skilled legislator, Crockett added a certain amount of frontier color to Congress. Contrary to his portrayal in the old Disney TV series, Crockett never wore his buckskin suit and coonskin cap on the House floor, although he was known for taking time off to go bear hunting.

After Crockett split with Jackson's Democratic Party, he was courted by the anti-Jacksonian Whigs. The Whigs played up Crockett's frontier background, hoping to offset Jackson's populist image.

When he lost his bid for reelection in 1834, Crockett told the voters, "You can go to hell and I will go to Texas." On March 6, 1836, Davy Crockett died in the defense of the Alamo. His body was burned by the victorious Mexican forces.

★ ★ ★

REVERSING A REJECTION

In 1834, the Senate rejected the nomination of Roger Taney of Maryland as Secretary of the Treasury. It was the first time the Senate rejected a President's nomination for a Cabinet position.

Sam Houston helped found the
Republic of Texas, served as its
president, helped bring it into the
Union, represented the state in the
U.S. Senate, and, finally, returned
to Texas to serve as its governor.

PHOTO CREDIT:
Library of Congress
Neg. no. LC-USZ62-110029

The Senators must have changed their opinion about Taney over the next two years. In 1836 the Senate approved Taney's nomination to be Chief Justice of the United States, a position he held for the next 28 years.

★ ★ ★

The President of Texas

One of the most colorful characters to serve in Congress, was Sam Houston. Texas was an independent nation when it joined the Union in 1845, and Sam Houston was its President, so he is the only former president of a foreign country to serve in Congress.

Born in Tennessee, Houston represented that state in the House from 1823 to 1827 and served as Governor of Tennessee from 1827 to 1829. He later moved to Texas, where he helped found the Republic of Texas and win its independence from Mexico. When Texas was admitted to the Union as the 28th state, Houston was elected to the U.S. Senate.

A flamboyant personality, Houston often wore a panther-skin vest to the Senate. At times, he would show up wearing a Mexican sombrero and wrapped in a blanket. He was also known to whittle during Senate debates, and would send hearts, birds or other small wooden figures up to ladies in the gallery.

Houston strongly supported the Union and his state's place in it. He was attacked by fellow Southerners for supporting Henry Clay's Compromise of 1850 and for opposing the Kansas-Nebraska Act of 1854. The Texas legislature voted to recall him from the Senate in 1857.

Still, Sam Houston was not the kind of man who could be kept down for long. In 1859, he was elected Governor of Texas. Houston ran as an independent, and, without the help of a party organization or sympathetic newspapers, he won on the strength of his character, personality and reputation.

As governor, he continued his unswerving loyalty to the Union, and refused to entertain the idea of his state's secession. He was removed from office when he refused to take an oath of loyalty to the Confederacy.

In *Profiles in Courage*, John F. Kennedy wrote that Sam Houston was a man of contradictions:

"He was fiercely ambitious, yet at the end he sacrificed for principle all he had ever won or wanted. He was a Southerner, and yet he steadfastly maintained his loyalty to the Union. He was a slaveholder who defended the right of Northern ministers to petition Congress against slavery; he was a notorious drinker who took the vow of temperance; he was an adopted son of the Cherokee Indians who won his first military honors fighting the Creeks; he was a Governor of Tennessee, but a Senator from Texas. He was in turn magnanimous yet vindictive, affectionate yet cruel, eccentric yet self-conscious, faithful yet optimistic. But Sam Houston's contradictions actually confirm his

one basic, consistent quality: indomitable individualism, sometimes spectacular, sometimes crude, sometimes mysterious, but always courageous. He could be all things to all men—and yet, when faced with his greatest challenge, he was faithful to himself and to Texas. The turmoil within Sam Houston was nothing more than the turmoil which racked the United States in those stormy years before the Civil War, the colorful uniqueness of Sam Houston was nothing more than the primitive expression of the frontier he had always known."

Houston died two years later. His last words called out to his beloved wife, Margaret, and his beloved Texas.

Mark Twain Goes to Washington

Humorist and author Mark Twain loved to poke fun at authority, and Congress was an easy target for him.

"It could probably be shown by facts and figures that there is no distinctly native American criminal class except Congress," Twain wrote in 1897.

Twain's observations of Congress date back to 1853, when, at age 18 and still known by his given name of Samuel Clemens, he traveled the country and chronicled his travels in letters to his brother, Orion. Orion was the publisher of the Muscatine, Iowa, *Journal* and printed young Sam's letters in his paper.

Among the writer's observations of Congress:

"The Senate is now composed of a different material from what it once was. Its glory hath departed. Its halls no longer echo the words of Clay, or Webster, or Calhoun..."

"The Senators dress very plainly, as they should, and all avoid display and do not speak unless they have something to say—and that cannot be said of the Representatives."

"In the House, nearly every man seemed to have something weighing on his mind on which the salvation of the Republic depended, and which he appeared very anxious to ease himself of; and so there were generally half a dozen of them on the floor, and 'Mr. Chairman! Mr. Chairman!' was echoed from every part of the House."

"Mr. Benton sits silent and gloomy in the midst of the din (in the House Chamber), *like a lion imprisoned in a cage of monkeys, who, feeling his superiority, disdains to notice their chattering."*

(This is a reference to Thomas Hart Benton, long-time Senator from Missouri, who finished his political career with a single term in the House.)

Devil Dan

When Congressman Dan Sickles of New York and his wife came to Washington in 1857, they found a home off Lafayette Square near the White House. Sickles, an ambitious young man of 37, was so consumed with his career that he did not notice his wife's unhappiness. Teresa Sickles, 15 years younger than her husband, engaged in a rather public affair with Phillip Barton Key, son of Francis Scott Key, author of *The Star Spangled Banner*.

When Dan Sickles learned of the affair, he could not control his rage. On that February day in 1859, in a fit of jealousy, Sickles armed himself with three pistols and went out in search of his wife's lover. He found Key on the street near Lafayette Square. In broad daylight, and in front of witnesses, Sickles shot Key twice, the second and fatal shot at point-blank range.

Most Washingtonians expected Sickles to hang for the deed. He didn't. Sickles became the first

accused murderer in American history to beat a murder rap by using the plea "not guilty by reason of temporary insanity."

A few years later, Sickles left Congress to fight in the Civil War. He went on to earn the rank of major general in the Union Army. He won the Medal of Honor for his actions at the Battle of Gettysburg, where he lost a leg to a Confederate cannonball. Sickles donated the shattered leg bone to the Army Medical Museum. After the war, Sickles was said to visit the museum frequently, often bringing out-of-town visitors to see his leg.

He served one more term in Congress late in life and died at the ripe old age of 95.

Congressional Champions

In 1858, John Morrissey was the heavyweight boxing champion of the world. From 1867 to 1871, he served in Congress as a Representative from New York.

Morrissey was the first professional athlete to be elected to Congress. Over the years, others have turned their fame on the field of play into a career in politics.

Here are some of the more notable sportsmen to come to Congress:

Ralph Metcalfe, Illinois (House 1971-78): Sprinter Metcalfe won silver and bronze medals in the 1932 Olympic Games in Los Angeles. In the 1936 games in Berlin, teammate Jesse Owens and Metcalfe stunned German Chancellor Adolf Hitler when they finished first and second, respectively, in the 100-yard dash. Metcalfe and Owens also teamed up to win the gold in the 4 x 100 relay. USA Track and Field enshrined Metcalfe in its Hall of Fame in 1975.

Jack Kemp, New York (House 1971-1989): Kemp spent 13 seasons as a quarterback in the American Football League. In 1960, he led the league in passing. In 1964 and 1965, he quarterbacked the Buffalo Bills to successive AFL championships. Kemp was named Most Valuable Player in the 1965 championship game. He was elected to the House in 1970

and later served as Secretary of Housing and Urban Development under George H.W. Bush. In 1996, Kemp ran unsuccessfully for Vice President on the Republican ticket with Sen. Robert J. Dole.

Bill Bradley, New Jersey (Senate 1979-1997): As a student at Princeton University, Bradley won a Rhodes Scholarship. As a member of the U.S. Olympic basketball team in 1964, he won a gold medal. As a New York Knick, Bradley won National Basketball Association championships in 1970 and 1973. In 1978, he won a seat in the U.S. Senate. In 1982, Bradley won induction into the Basketball Hall of Fame.

Jim Bunning, Kentucky (House 1987-1999; Senate 1999-): A right-handed pitcher for 17 seasons in the major leagues, Bunning was known for his menacing side-arm delivery. He notched 224 wins, mostly with the Detroit Tigers and Philadelphia Phillies. He pitched a perfect game—not allowing a single runner to reach base—in 1964. Bunning was the first pitcher since the legendary Cy Young to register 100 wins and 1,000 strikeouts in both the National and American Leagues. When he retired from the sport in 1971, he was second only to another legend, Walter Johnson, on the all-time strikeout list. Bunning was enshrined in the Baseball Hall of Fame in 1996.

Steve Largent, Oklahoma (House 1994-2002): For 13 seasons, Largent was the go-to receiver for the Seattle Seahawks. Although he led the National Football League in receptions in only two seasons, 1979 and 1985, his consistent performance throughout his career put Largent at the top of the league's receivers in lifetime performance by the time he retired in 1989. In 1995, Largent was inducted into the Pro Football Hall of Fame.

Jim Ryun, Kansas (House 1996-): Jim Ryun set the record for the mile run for male high school runners in 1965. His time of 3:55.3 stood unbroken for 36 years. In 1966, at the age of 19, Ryun set the world record in the mile run, 3 minutes, 51.3 seconds. A year later, he bettered his own mark by two-tenths of a second. Ryun also set records in the 1500 meter and 880 meter runs. He made the U.S. Olympic track and field team in 1964 while still in high school. He won a silver medal in the mile run at the 1968 games, but fell during the championship heat and finished out of contention in 1972. In 1980, Ryun was inducted into USA Track and Field's Hall of Fame.

★ ★ ★

SOUP'S ON!

Bean soup is served every day in the House and Senate restaurants. This tradition dates back to the early 20th Century, but its exact origins are cloudy. Some say the soup earned a permanent spot on the menu thanks to the influence of Sen. Fred Thomas Dubois of Idaho. Other accounts credit Sen. Knute Nelson of Minnesota, while still others say it was House Speaker Joe Cannon of Illinois. Whatever its history, the thick concoction has nourished a century's worth of hungry legislators.

Here is the recipe for Senate Bean Soup, courtesy of the Senate Historical Office. The House restaurants serve a vegetarian version of the soup.

Ingredients:
2 pounds dried navy pea beans
4 quarts hot water
1-1/2 pounds smoked ham hocks
1 onion chopped
2 tablespoons butter
salt and pepper

Directions: Wash and run hot water through the beans until slightly whitened. Place beans in pot with four quarts of hot water. Add ham hocks and boil for three hours. Set aside to cool. Dice meat and return to soup. Lightly brown the chopped onion in butter and add to soup. Bring to a boil, then season with salt and pepper. Serves eight.

★ ★ ★

It'll Never Get Off the Ground

In a speech to the house in 1899, Rep. John F. Fitzgerald of Massachusetts, grandfather of President John F. Kennedy, spoke of the wondrous inventions of the 19th Century, which included the telephone, electric lighting and the automobile. He wondered aloud what new technologies the next hundred years would bring, and speculated that by the end of the 20th Century, Americans would travel the world "on ships that would fly through the air."

The House laughed at Fitzgerald's prediction.

Four years later, the Wright Brothers made their first successful flight.

Twenty-eight years later, Charles Lindbergh flew solo from New York to Paris.

Seventy years later, astronauts Neil Armstrong and Edwin Aldrin planted the American flag on the moon.

One hundred years later, U.S. airlines carried 636 million passengers, nearly nine times the population of the entire country in 1899, to domestic and foreign destinations "on ships that would fly through the air."

SERVING UP THE SOUP

Cooks in the Senate restaurant prepare another batch of Senate Bean Soup, a daily menu item in the Senate restaurants for the past century.

PHOTO CREDIT:
U.S. Senate Historical Office

Freshman Hazing

If you're ever elected to the United States Senate,
don't let it go to your head. Senior Senators have
a history of hazing new arrivals, especially those
who might come to the office with an inflated
sense of self-importance.

One such hazing victim was Robert La Follette
of Wisconsin. A leader in the Progressive movement in the early 20th Century, LaFollette came to
Washington with much fanfare. The Senate leadership decided to teach the uppity freshman some
humility. First they gave him an office in the
Capitol basement next to the boiler room.
Then they assigned him to the Committee on
the Improvement of the Potomac Riverfront,
which hadn't met since before the Civil War.

When Thomas Kearns of Utah came to the
Senate in 1901, he was a self-made, wealthy
businessman. Although he never finished
high school, Kearns had built a successful
mining business and had been a delegate to
his state's constitutional convention.

Kearns' reputation as someone who lacked
formal education but made up for it with
"horse sense," reached the ear of Sen.
Chauncey Depew of New York. Depew was a
graduate of Yale, a successful lawyer, former
president of the New York Central Hudson
River Railroad Co., and once ran for President
of the United States. He was unimpressed
with Kearns' accomplishments.

"[Horse sense] may be all right in Utah,"
Depew said, "but the United States Senate is not a
stable."

Sen. Samuel Shortridge of California got a taste
of this tradition even before he was elected to the
Senate in 1921. Shortridge served as a Republican
Presidential Elector in the elections of 1888, 1900,
and 1908, and, following one of the elections, was
delegated the task of delivering California's electoral votes to Washington.

Imbued with his own importance for earning
such a lofty responsibility, Shortridge zealously
guarded the sacred ballots on the long cross-
country train ride. When he arrived at the
Capitol, Shortridge insisted on being shown to the
office of the Senate's President Pro Tem, William
P. Frye of Maine. Shortridge marched into Frye's
office and announced loudly that he was there to
present the Presidential electoral votes from
California to the U.S. Congress.

Frye, unimpressed, responded dryly, "All right
Mr. Stockbridge. Throw your box over there on
the table with the rest of the ballots."

He Should Have
Ordered the Bean Soup

Never order eggnog on a hot day. That is the les-
son that La Follette learned during a floor speech
in 1908. On a hot afternoon in late May, the
Wisconsin Republican was in the midst of a filibuster when he asked for a glass of eggnog from
the Senate kitchen. When the drink arrived, La
Follette took one taste and immediately ordered it
removed. "Take it away. It's drugged," La Follette
said.

The contents were later analyzed and found to
contain ptomaine, a poisonous contaminant often
found in spoiled or improperly prepared food.
Had the Senator finished the glass of eggnog, the
results could have been fatal.

Cigar Stories

Thomas Riley Marshall served as Vice President under President Woodrow Wilson (1913-1921). A former Governor of Indiana, Marshall was uncomfortable in his secondary role in the federal government. One day while presiding over a rather boring session of the Senate, Marshall got tired of hearing Senators expound on what the country needed.

Finally, an exasperated Vice President Marshall chimed in, "What this country needs is a good five-cent cigar!"

In 1997, Sen. Kit Bond, a Republican from Missouri, went Marshall a nickel's worth better. A staffer for another Senator noticed a pair of cigars in Bond's coat pocket and hoped to get a good smoking tip.

"What kind of cigars do you smoke, Senator?" the aide asked.

Bond replied with a chuckle. "Free ones!" he said.

Breaking the Gender Barrier

Jeanette Rankin of Montana was a leader in the study of women's issues and the fight for women's rights. In 1915 she moved to New Zealand and worked as a seamstress in order to examine firsthand the social and working conditions experienced by women there. A year later, she returned to the States to become the first woman elected to the U.S. Congress, four years before the 20th Amendment guaranteed women in the United States the right to vote.

A devoted pacifist, Rep. Rankin raised eyebrows when she opposed the declaration of war against Germany in April, 1917. In 1918, Rep. Rankin did not seek renomination to her House seat. Instead she became the first woman to run, though unsuccessfully, for a seat in the U.S. Senate.

Rep. Rankin returned to Congress in 1941. Again, war loomed for the United States. Following the Japanese attack on Pearl Harbor, President Roosevelt asked Congress to vote for a declaration of war against Japan. As she had done 24 years earlier, Rep. Rankin opposed the declaration. She could not vote for war.

Rep. Rankin retired from Congress in 1943, but continued to be an activist for social justice and women's rights until her death in 1973.

Had Rankin not stuck to her pacifist principles and voted with the majority to declare war on Germany in 1917, she might have broken the gender barrier in the Senate as well. But, with Rankin's defeat in the elections of 1918, that task was left for others.

Rebecca Latimore Felton of Georgia served in the Senate for just 24 hours, but made history nonetheless. On November 21, 1922, she became the first woman to serve in the United States Senate.

Sen. Felton was appointed by Gov. Thomas Hardwick to serve out the term of the late Thomas E. Waters. Hardwick, who had opposed giving the vote to women, was under much pressure from female voters to appoint a woman to the seat. Hardwick made the appointment on October 3, but did not expect the appointee to serve. The Senate had adjourned for the year and an election in November would fill the seat for the next Congress.

The Governor did not expect Congress to meet in a special session, which it did in late November. On November 21, Sen. Felton took the oath of office. The next day she made a speech on the Senate floor. And resigned.

Sen. Felton's newly elected successor, Walter E. George, was sworn in immediately after Felton's speech, and took her place in the Senate.

"I CANNOT VOTE FOR WAR"

Jeannette Rankin of Montana was the first woman elected to Congress and the first woman to run for a seat in the U.S. Senate. A pacifist, Rankin voted against declaring war in both World War I and World War II.

PHOTO CREDIT:
Jeff Lesnik

After her brief term in the Senate, Sen. Felton continued to write and lecture on women's rights issues. She died in 1930 at age 94.

Sen. Felton holds the record for the shortest term of service in the Senate, and, at age 87, she is the oldest person—at the time of first swearing in—to take a seat in the Senate.

The Widow's Mandate

When a Senator or Representative dies in office, his wife is often appointed or elected to serve out his unexpired term. This has become known as the Widow's Mandate. (So far, no female Members of Congress have been succeeded by their husbands, so there is no corresponding Widower's Mandate. Yet.)

Since 1923, eight women have been appointed to the U.S. Senate in this way. The first, Sen. Hattie Caraway of Arkansas (1931-1941), was appointed following the death of her husband, Sen. Thaddeus H. Caraway. She went on to win the special election to fill out his term, and was reelected two more times. She became the first woman to win election to the Senate, and, at 14 years, she was the longest serving of the Senate widows.

Unlike the other widows who came to the Senate by appointment, Sen. Maurine Brown Neuberger of Oregon (1960-67) did it the hard way. She was not appointed to the seat vacated by her deceased husband, Sen. Richard L. Neuberger, but won a special election to succeed him, then won reelection to a full term.

The most recent widow, Sen. Jean Carnahan, was appointed to the Senate following the posthumous election of her husband, Missouri Governor Mel Carnahan. Mel Carnahan never served in the Senate, so it could not be said that his widow succeeded him in office. Also, Missouri voters knew

in advance that Jean Carnahan would be appointed if her late husband won the election, so, in a way, Jean Carnahan won the election even though her husband's name was on the ballot. (More on this election later.)

In the House, 37 women succeeded their late husbands in office. Unlike the Senate, no one can be appointed to the House, so all 37 came to Congress by winning elections.

Rep. Mae Ella Nolan of California was the first woman to follow her husband to Congress, and served nearly two years. Her husband, John Ignatius Nolan, had died just a few weeks after winning reelection in 1922. Mae Ella Nolan won the special election to fill out her husband's term in January of 1923. She did not seek reelection in 1924.

The longest serving widow in the House is Rep. Frances Payne Bolton, who won a special election to succeed her husband, Chester C. Bolton of Ohio, in 1940. She served 29 years, and retired in 1969 after losing reelection to a 16th term.

Like many of the women who came to Congress under the Widow's Mandate, Margaret Chase Smith of Maine established herself as a formidable legislator in her own right. After winning a special election to fill out the term of her late husband, Clyde H. Smith, she served nine years in the House. In 1948, Margaret Chase Smith was elected to the Senate, where she served four terms. At the Republican National Convention in 1964, Sen. Smith became the first woman in American history to have her name placed in nomination for President at a major political party convention. She retired in 1972, after 33 years in Congress, when she lost a bid for a fifth Senate term.

Finally, Rep. Leonor K. Sullivan of Missouri did not succeed her husband directly. Rep. John B. Sullivan died in 1951. His widow lost the special election to succeed him, but was elected to Congress in her own right the following year. She served for 25 years.

FIRST ELECTED

In 1932, Hattie Caraway of Arkansas became the first woman elected to the Senate. She would serve 12 more years. Her portrait, by John Oliver Buckley, hangs outside the Senate Chamber.

Dishing the dirt

Nicholas Longworth served as Speaker of the House from 1925 through 1931, and a House office building is named after him. But Longworth may be best known for his wife, Alice, the daughter of President Theodore Roosevelt. Alice Roosevelt Longworth was a prominent Washington socialite and an incurable gossip. She is reported to have owned an embroidered pillow carrying the message, "If you can't say something good about some one, sit right here next to me."

CONGRESSIONAL BOOTLEGGER

The 18th Amendment to the Constitution, which was ratified in 1919 and took effect a year later, banned the manufacture, sale or transportation of intoxicating liquors in the United States. That didn't stop a number of Members of Congress from taking a nip now and then.

To supply them with spirits, the Congressmen turned to one George C. Cassiday. In short order, Cassiday was busy running rum for Rep-

resentatives. He became known by the green felt hat he always wore.

Cassiday's service to the House lasted until 1925 before the Capitol Police shut him down. He then moved over to the Senate side, where he operated for another four years until Vice President Charles Curtis and the Secretary of the Senate decided something had to be done. They staged a sting operation using a young Prohibition agent named Roger Butts. Cassiday was arrested and served a short jail term. Butts became known as the "Dry Spy."

The 21st Amendment ended Prohibition in 1933, and put Cassiday out of business for good.

The Car Pool

Despite their party differences, Speaker Longworth was fast friends with his Democratic counterpart in the House, Minority Leader John Nance Garner of Texas. The two men were so close that they often rode home from work together in the Speaker's official car. Garner often needled Longworth that he should take good care of the car, because, if power in the House should shift to the Democrats, Garner would be elected Speaker and take custody of the vehicle.

In the elections of 1930, control of the House hung in the balance. Longworth and Garner retired for the night with several seats undecided and the majority of the House in doubt. The would be in charge of the House in the next Congress. Longworth wired Garner the question, "Whose car is it?

Garner wired back that he expected the Democrats to win the majority, so the car

would be his, but he'd be happy to let Longworth continue to ride with him. When all the votes were tallied, though, the Democrats fell short of a majority and the Republicans continued to control the House by the slimmest of margins. It took a number of deaths among the Republican membership of the House, including Longworth's, over the next 13 months to give Garner and his party control and make Garner Speaker of the House, and custodian of the car.

Sound and Light

The floodlit dome of the Capitol is a stunning and familiar sight in the nighttime Washington skyline, but over the years a number of alternative ideas have been floated for illuminating the Capitol. For better or worse, these ideas have gone nowhere.

One such suggestion arose in 1936, when Karl L. Gower, who listed his address as the Central YMCA in Washington, sent a letter to Rep. Jennings Randolph of West Virginia, suggesting that the Capitol, Washington Monument and Lincoln Memorial be outlined with red neon lights.

The red lines would give the buildings a distinctive, modern look, Gower wrote, while making them highly visible to aircraft, especially in fog or rain. He said the glass tubes holding the neon gas would be inconspicuous during the day and therefore would not detract from the appearance of the buildings.

Thirty years later, in 1966, Rep. Henry Reuss of Wisconsin proposed a sound and light show for the Capitol. Inspired by such shows in France, Reuss suggested using dramatic lighting on the building timed to recorded music and narration to tell the building's—and the nation's—history.

Reuss said Congress could provide a "tremendously impressive show at low cost."

Congress disagreed, and the proposal was dropped.

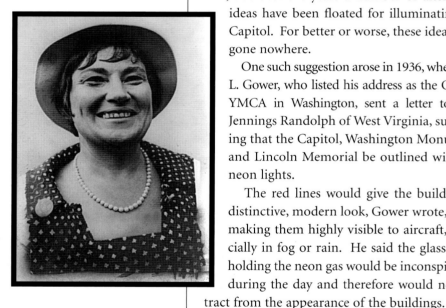

Fishbait Miller

He told Henry Kissinger to "git." He annoyed Richard Nixon. Lyndon Johnson wanted him; Sam Rayburn said he couldn't have him. He tried to make Bella Abzug take off her hat. He announced VIP visitors to the House Chamber with a booming "Mistah Speakaaah..."

His name was William "Fishbait" Miller, and he served as House Doorkeeper from 1949 to 1953 and again from 1955 to 1974. He held the post of Minority Housekeeper when the Republicans controlled the House in 1947-49 and 1953-55.

Miller came to the Capitol in 1933 from his native Mississippi under the patronage of Rep. William Colmer of Pascagoula. He started out as a clerk in the House Post Office and eventually worked his way up the leadership ladder to Doorkeeper.

Miller was known for his outgoing, outspoken manner. He would greet female staffers with a kiss and promise to find them rich husbands. He would babysit Members' children. According to his 1989 obituary in *The Washington Post*, one critic said Miller "turned obsequiousness into an art form."

When the future Queen of England, Princess Elizabeth, and her husband, Prince Philip, visited the House Chamber in 1952, Miller greeted her with a friendly, "Howdy, Ma'am." Later, as the Princess stood waving from the Speaker's Rostrum, Fishbait boomed to his assistant, "Hey, pass me up the Prince."

During his time as Doorkeeper, Miller announced every President from Harry Truman through Gerald Ford. Vice President Lyndon Johnson told Speaker and fellow Texan Sam Rayburn that he wanted Miller on his staff. Rayburn refused.

One of Miller's most famous adversaries was Rep. Bella Abzug of New York. Rep. Abzug was never seen without a broad-brimmed hat that had be come her signature. In 1971, when the newly eleced Congresswoman went to step on the House floor for the first time, Miller blocked her way and reminded her of the House Rules, which prohibit the wearing of hats in the chamber. Fishbait lost the argument and Rep. Abzug was never seen on the floor—House rules notwithstanding—without her hat.

When Ford was sworn in as Vice President before a joint session of Congress in the House Chamber in 1973, Miller noticed Secretary of State Henry Kissinger holding up the receiving line. Miller needed to prod Kissinger a bit to get the line moving again.

"I told him 'Henry, you got to git,'" Miller told *The Washington Star* in an interview a year later.

The year before, Richard Nixon was waiting to enter the chamber to address Congress and report on his landmark trip to the Soviet Union. Miller greeted the President warmly and asked many questions about the Presidential trip. An irritated Nixon complained to Ford, who was then the Minority Leader of the House. Ford told Nixon, "Fishbait came here before we did and he's going to be here when we're gone."

By the end of 1974, the time for Miller's retirement had come. His patron, Rep. Colmer, retired in 1972 after three terms as the chairman of the powerful Rules Committee. Miller's style of the back-slapping Southern country boy politician was out of step with the post-Watergate Congress.

Ford's prediction nearly came true. By the time Miller retired, Nixon had left office in disgrace and was replaced by Ford. Ford would be voted out of office two years later.

Right up to the end of his service, however, Miller never hesitated to provide an occasional tour or helpful directions to Capitol visitors. He told the *Star* that he always remembered what Rayburn had told him years before: These people are the ones who pay the bills that keep the place running.

Nice line, though

In 1947, the House Un-American Activities Committee was engaged in hearings to root out Communist influences in the entertainment industry. Writer Ring Lardner, who by that time was doing screenplays for the movies, was called in to testify about Communists working in Hollywood.

Chairman J. Parnell Thomas of New Jersey asked Lardner if he himself had ever been a member of the Communist Party. Like many others who were questioned by the committee, Lardner chose not to answer the question.

"I could answer [the question], but I would hate myself in the morning," Lardner replied.

Unfortunately, Lardner did not specifically base his refusal to answer on the rights bestowed by the Fifth Amendment to the Constitution. He was found in contempt of Congress and served a year in a federal pen.

★ ★ ★

THE ANTELOPE SITUATION

Sen. Eugene P. Millikin of Colorado frequently used the phrase "the antelope situation" to describe the Senate's actions when facing a tough decision.

Millikin, who served in the Senate from 1945 through 1957, said that the Senate often resembled antelope, who one moment can be oberserved grazing quietly and the next moment in full flight, their white tails pointed skyward.

According to An American Bestiary *by Sen. Eugene J. McCarthy, Millikin could sense when the Senate was facing such a situation, and would tell his fellow Senators, "The antelope time has come. There is nothing for us to do but paint a white stripe on the seat of our pants, panic and vote with the unity of a herd of antelope taking flight."*

★ ★ ★

The Atomic Capitol

In 1956, Sen. Clinton P. Anderson of New Mexico and Rep. W. Sterling Cole of New York introduced legislation to bring the Capitol into the atomic age. Literally.

The two legislators proposed that the electric power and steam heat for the Capitol complex be provided by nuclear power. Their bill would have authorized $200,000 to finance a study on refitting the Capitol's power plant for this purpose.

The bill went nowhere. Today, the Capitol is heated by steam from the power plant, and electrical service comes from the local utility.

Senators to the Stars

On February 20, 1962, Astronaut John Glenn became the third American to travel in outer space, and the first to orbit the globe.

Back on earth, Glenn entered politics, winning a seat in the United States Senate on his second try in 1974. In 1984, he made an unsuccessful run for the Democratic Presidential nomination.

On October 29, 1998, Glenn made history a second time, returning to space at age 77. His first flight, alone aboard the Mercury capsule *Friendship 7*, lasted just five hours. His second flight, with six other astronauts aboard the space shuttle *Discovery*, covered nine days and provided scientists with valuable data on the effects of space travel on the aging.

Glenn is not the only Senator to travel in space. In 1985, Sen. Jake Garn of Utah spent a week as a mission specialist aboard the *Discovery*. Future Sen. Bill Nelson of Florida made the trip aboard the shuttle *Columbia* in 1986. At the time, Nelson was serving in the House and was chairman of the Subcommittee on Space.

ASTRONAUT, SENATOR, HERO

Sen. John Glenn of Ohio was the first American to orbit the earth and, later, the oldest American to fly in space.

PHOTO CREDIT: NASA

GOD IS MY COPILOT

In 1957, after returning from a religious convocation in Honolulu, the Senate Chaplain, the Rev. Frederick Brown Harris, told a hair-raising story about his trip.

At one point on the return flight, one of the plane's four engines gave out. As the flight attendant went around reassuring passengers that everything was all right and they would just arrive a little later than scheduled, the Rev. Brown offered her some reassurance of his own. The chaplain told her not to worry, because there were eight bishops on board. The flight attendant said she would relay the information to the captain.

When she returned from the cockpit, Rev. Brown asked her what the captain had to say.

"He said he'd rather have four engines," she replied.

Gimme Shelter

The development of the atomic bomb added a new word to the popular dictionary: *fallout*. Fallout is radioactive dust that is kicked up by a nuclear explosion and carried by the wind to other areas of the world.

To protect against the effects of this radioactive dust, the government established fallout shelters in the basements of schools and other public buildings throughout the country. While the shelters could not protect their occupants from the blast of a nuclear weapon, they could help shield the population from radioactive fallout.

A 1963 report in *The Washington Post* said the Architect of the Capitol estimated some 36,000 people could be accommodated in fallout shelters in the basements and garages of the Capitol and the House and Senate office buildings. (The figure in cluded about 12,000 who could be sheltered in the Rayburn building, which was still under construction at the time.)

Yellow and black Fallout Shelter signs were placed throughout the complex, directing people to the safe areas. With the end of the Cold War, the signs have slowly disappeared. One notable exception: a sign still hangs in the area of Washington's tomb below the Crypt, designating the area as an official Fallout Shelter.

Gimme Even More Shelter

While Capitol Hill staffers and neighbors could take shelter from fallout in the lower reaches of the Capitol complex, Members of Congress had a better deal going.

In 1956, Congress appointed a commission to look at ways to create additional space in the Capitol. One of the plans included the construction of a bomb shelter under the West Lawn to house Congress if a nuclear war broke out. The commission's study led to the extension of the East Front, but a bomb shelter at the Capitol was not included in the final plans.

Instead, a secret shelter was built in the hills of West Virginia, adjacent to the luxurious Greenbrier resort. Constructed in 1959, at the height of the Cold War, the facility was a closely guarded secret. Even most Members of Congress weren't aware of its existence, until *The Washington Post* exposed the shelter in 1992.

The facility was no secret to many in the nearby town of White Sulphur Springs, West Virginia. According to the *Post* story, the Defense Department sent two men who knew nothing about the shelter out to White Sulphur Springs to casually ask around and see what they could find out. The two came back loaded with enough details that the Pentagon had to issue them security clearances.

Reinforced with 50,000 tons of concrete, the facility provided meeting chambers for both the House and Senate and living facilities for Members and a small staff. (No spouses or children.)

When the story broke, Speaker Thomas Foley and the rest of Congressional leadership asked the Pentagon to close the site. The Greenbrier now offers guided tours of the facility to its guests and the general public.

Following the terrorist attacks on the World Trade Center and the Pentagon in 2001, new concerns arose about the ability of the House and Senate to function in time of a national emergency. The search began for a new secret, secure site to shelter Congress.

A Capitol Dress Code?

People on vacation dress for comfort. That fact discomforted Rep. Walter McVey.

In 1961, the Kansas Republican introduced legislation in the House Public Works Committee to set a dress code for visitors to the U.S. Capitol.

Under McVey's bill, adults and teenagers wearing shorts would be barred from the Capitol. Only children under 12 would be allowed to bare their legs in the building.

McVey said he introduced the bill to restore dignity to the Capitol.

When Speaker Sam Rayburn was asked his opinion about tourists wearing shorts, he withheld comment. "I haven't examined all of them yet," he said.

Rep. Kathryn Granahan agreed with McVey. She said she found the proliferation of short pants among Capitol visitors to be "perfectly dreadful, nauseating, disgraceful."

Still, the bill went nowhere, much to the relief of the thousands of tourists who visit the Capitol during the hot, muggy Washington summers.

By 2001, Capitol Police officers on outdoor duty were allowed to wear shorts as part of their uniform. Officers working inside the air-conditioned Capitol and office buildings still have to wear long pants.

SAFETY ZONE

Fallout Shelter signs were once common throughout the Capitol complex.

PHOTO CREDIT:
Jeff Lesnik

The Great Desk Compromise

When Sen. Strom Thurmond of South Carolina switched his loyalty from the Democratic to Republican Party in 1964, he wanted to use the desk once occupied by fellow South Carolinian John C. Calhoun. The Democrats had other ideas.

Thurmond thought he had been using Calhoun's desk all along, but he was mistaken. Calhoun's desk had also been used by Sen. Huey Long of Louisiana, and was now in the possession of Sen. Russell Long, Huey's son. Russell did not want to give it up, especially to a Senator who had just bolted from his party.

A compromise was struck. In a trade worthy of a trio of NFL teams on draft day, Long traded desks with Sen. Clinton P. Anderson of New Mexico. Anderson's desk had been used by Long's mother, Rose McConnell Long, when she was appointed to the Senate following his father's death. (The three Longs are the only husband-wife-son combination to have served in the Senate, so far.)

Anderson then traded the Calhoun desk to the Senator from South Carolina—not Thurmond, but the other Senator from the state, Olin D. Johnston, a Democrat. When Johnston died in office in 1965, the desk passed to his successor, Ernest F. Hollings.

Thurmond would serve in the Senate for 38 more years, but he would never lay claim to Calhoun's desk.

⸻ ★★★ ⸻

LIGHTS, BELLS AND BUZZERS

Visitors to Capitol Hill while Congress is in session are often startled to hear loud bells or buzzers sound in the middle of the day.

The alarms are part of a system that alerts Senators and Representatives to votes and other significant activities on the floor of the Senate or House. The bells (or buzzers, in offices and other parts of some buildings) are used in conjunction with light signals incorporated into clocks and light bars around the Hill.

The House and Senate each has its own alert system. In both the House and Senate systems, one long ring signals the beginning of the legislative day. A red light remains lit while the chamber is in session. Combinations of white lights signal quorum calls, recorded votes, recesses and other activities on the floor.

In the Capitol, the parts of the building north of the Rotunda use the Senate alert system, while the southern half of the building is on the House system. One room, EF-100, which is located in the center of the East Front, displays the Senate light bar on its north wall, and the House signals on its south wall.

Former Congressman Bradford Morse of New York once told of a group of constituents who heard the bells sound while visiting Morse's office. "What does that mean?" one constituent asked. "Maybe one of them escaped," guessed another.

The most ominous of the bell signals has never been used, except in tests. Six flashing lights and 12 rings of the bell alerts the complex to a nuclear attack.

⸻ ★★★ ⸻

DESK POLITICS (*above*)

The Senate Curator keeps track of which desk is used by which Senator over the years. Some of the desks used by famous former Senators have become highly coveted.

PHOTO CREDIT:
From the Collection of the Senate Curator

SIGNAL LIGHTS (*right*)

Senators and Representatives are alerted to votes and other activities in their respective chambers by signal lights and bells. The lights are often displayed on clocks in offices, meeting rooms and corridors of the Capitol and the nearby Congressional office buildings.

PHOTO CREDIT:
Jim Berard

Flower Power

In the early days of the Senate, it was not unusual for a Senator to receive flowers from an admirer, political supporter or a grateful constituent who had received a favor or service. Senators had no office space, so they would place the flowers on their desks in the Senate Chamber.

Soon, flowers on the desk became a status symbol for Senators, to the point that Senators would send flowers to themselves. As Senators tried to outdo each other, large bouquets began to take up so much space that the Senators themselves could not be seen for all the flowers. The Senate soon adopted rules banning flowers from the chamber.

One notable exception was allowed in 1968. Following the assassination of Democratic Sen. Robert F. Kennedy of New York, Sen. Margaret Chase Smith, a Republican from Maine, placed a rose on Kennedy's desk in the Senate Chamber. She placed a fresh rose on the desk each day until Kennedy's appointed successor, Charles Goodell, took office.

The Ugly Side of Politics

The struggle for civil rights took an ugly turn on the floor of the House on January 5, 1965.

The House was organizing itself for the new Congress, swearing in new Members and electing a Speaker. The day's business was under a cloud of controversy. Civil rights activists protested the seating of the delegation from Mississippi, claiming the November election had been fraudulent because African American voters in the state had not been treated fairly.

Suddenly, a white man in black-face makeup burst onto the House floor. Mocking the protests of the civil rights groups, the man demanded to be seated as part of the Mississippi delegation.

Police arrested Robert A. Lloyd, 20, a member of the American Nazi Party.

Race was at the center of another ugly incident in the Capitol five years later.

On February 25, 1970, less than two years after the assassination of Dr. Martin Luther King, Jr., tensions still ran hot along racial lines. Then, the Governor of Georgia brought them to the boiling point.

Gov. Lester G. Maddox made a name for himself in the 1960's as a restaurant owner who refused to serve black patrons. When a customer of color would try to defy his racist policy, Maddox would threaten him with an ax handle. In 1966, Maddox used his segregationist reputation to narrowly win the race for Governor of Georgia. The ax handle became the symbol of his defiant stand against racial integration and social progress. So much so, that Maddox would hand out autographed ax handles to admirers as souvenirs.

On that day in 1970, the Governor came to Capitol Hill. While having lunch in the Members' Dining Room in the House wing, Maddox was recognized by fellow diners. In turn, Maddox handed out autographed ax handles to his greeters.

This activity caught the eye of Rep. Charles Diggs of Michigan, one of only nine African-American Members of Congress at the time. Diggs was angered by Maddox giving out such a blatant symbol of racism in the Congressional dining room. Diggs confronted Maddox, who claimed the ax handles were only souvenirs and there was no harm in handing them out. About the same time, Speaker John McCormack of Massachusetts heard of Maddox's activity and passed the word for it to stop.

Maddox angrily paid for his meal and left the dining room, but resumed handing out the ax handles in the hallway outside. He finally stopped when a Capitol Police officer intervened.

The incident dominated debate on the House floor that afternoon, as Members stood up to condemn Maddox's actions, while some of the

Georgians in the House felt obligated to defend their Governor.

"Perhaps the ax handle is the symbol of justice in Georgia, perhaps it is not," said Rep. Robert L. Legett of California. "In any case, the ax handle is not yet the symbol of law and order in the United States. It is a symbol of hooliganism and the law of the jungle, and it is no less so in the hands of an elected official."

"I regret that the incident took place. I cannot condone it," said Rep. Fletcher Thompson of Georgia. "Yet, I cannot sit idly by and allow him (Maddox) to be given the status of persona non grata in the House dining room when they give the Governors of all states this right."

Observed Rep. Louis Stokes of Ohio, "History will record for all time that today, February 24, 1970, the doors of the House of Representatives restaurant swung open and that a fool walked in."

★ ★ ★

WHAT SO PROUDLY WE HAILED... FOR 30 SECONDS

Four flagpoles prominently display the American flag on the Capitol, but there are several more on the building's roof that are unseen from ground level.

These poles are atop the House wing, just south of the dome. The poles accommodate requests for flags flown over the Capitol.

Flag requests are handled by the Flag Office, a division of the Architect of the Capitol. Every day, flag staff—make that flag personnel—continuously run flags up the special poles, fly them for a full 30 seconds, then bring them down and box them up for return to the requesting Congressional office. The flag is shipped to the purchaser with a certificate verifying the date it was flown over the Capitol.

These flags are popular gifts to commemorate special occasions such as weddings, graduations, or milestone birthdays. They are also popular

with civic groups who provide them to local institutions such as schools, hospitals, churches and municipal governments.

Persons interested in obtaining a flag that has flown over the Capitol—albeit for 30 seconds—should contact their Congressional Representative or one of their state's two Senators for further information on sizes, prices and availability.

★ ★ ★

Posthumous Politics, Part I

In 1972, freshman Rep. Nick Begich represented Alaska in the House of Representatives. He was only the third person to hold that state's lone House seat since Alaska joined the Union in 1959. At the same time, Rep. Hale Boggs was a powerful force on Capitol Hill. A 13-term Congressman from Louisiana, Boggs held the post of Majority Leader, second only to Speaker Carl Albert in the House

In October of that year, Begich was campaigning for reelection. He invited Boggs to campaign with him and help him win a second term. Boggs accepted the invitation. On October 20, 1972, Boggs and Begich boarded a twin engine plane in Anchorage for a flight to a campaign event in Juneau, the state capital. The plane disappeared en route.

FLAG CERTIFICATE

Flags that have flown over the Capitol come with a certificate verifying the date the flag was raised.

Boggs' widow, Lindy, ran for the vacant seat and won the right to succeed her husband in the House. Lindy Boggs served in Congress for 18 years. In 1997, President Clinton appointed her ambassador to the Vatican, a post she held until 2001.

★ ★ ★

ALASKA BIG AND SMALL

At 663,267 square miles, Alaska is the largest state in the Union by area. With 626,932 people, it is also one of the smallest states in population. Only Wyoming, Vermont and the District of Columbia are smaller.

Its sparse population entitles Alaska to only one Representative in the House. So, along with being the largest state in the Union, Alaska also holds the distinction of being the largest single Congressional District in the country.

★ ★ ★

The Lady With a Pipe

Rep. Millicent Fenwick was unusual in many ways. She was a woman in Congress when only a handful of seats were held by women. She was a smoker, when smoking was going out of style, and she smoked a pipe. Although Rep. Fenwick usually puffed on her pipe in her office, she often carried it with her to committee meetings and to votes on the House floor.

A former model for *Harper's Bazaar* and editor for *Vogue* magazine, Rep. Fenwick won her first term in Congress at age 64. She worked long hours and answered constituent mail with handwritten notes. Her combination of finishing school charm and New Jersey gumption earned her many admirers. Cartoonist Gary Trudeau used Rep. Fenwick as his model for the character of Congresswoman Lacey Davenport in his comic strip *Doonesbury.*

Despite a massive search effort, using the latest technology, no trace was ever found of the plane or its passengers. When Election Day arrived a few weeks after the disappearance, Boggs' and Begich's names appeared on the ballot in their respective states. Both won reelection.

By the time Congress reconvened in January, 1973, the search had ended and both men had been declared dead. The House ruled both seats vacant and called for special elections to fill them.

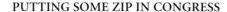

A Fiery Speaker

Speaker Jim Wright was known as a skilled orator, but one day, while posing for a photograph, the fire wasn't in Wright's words. It was in his hair.

At the time, when he was still just another Member of Congress, Wright sat on the House Public Works and Transportation Committee and chaired its Subcommittee on Investigations and Oversight. The subcommittee was looking into a new safety device for commercial aircraft: fireproof hoods that would protect passengers from smoke and flames as they escaped from a burning plane.

Parade magazine was covering the smoke hood issue and wanted to interview Wright for the article. The magazine also wanted a dramatic photo to go with the story. It was decided that the Parade photographer would snap a shot of Wright wearing one of the hoods. On an airplane. And there had to be fire.

Wright went along with the scheme. An aide dropped by a Capitol Hill hardware store and picked up a blowtorch. The Congressman, the aide and the photographer met a few blocks from the Capitol at Union Station for the shoot. (They had decided that the interior of an Amtrak coach would look enough like the cabin of an airliner for the purposes of the photo.)

Wright's long-time chief of staff, Marshall L. Lynam, described the scene in his memoir, *Stories I Never Told the Speaker.* "With confidence born of having survived both World War II air combat in the Pacific and one term in the Texas Legislature, Jim Wright gamely pulled the hood over his head. From inside came muffled words that sounded as if he were saying he was ready. Or maybe, in retrospect, he was saying, please pull down the hood a little further in the back," Lynam wrote.

The aide fired up the torch and brought the flame to the Congressman's head.

And set his boss's hair on fire.

The aide and the photographer were able to tamp out the flames before much damage was done. Once the fire was out, Wright gamely replaced the hood for a second take. This time Wright made sure the hood covered his whole head and neck.

The photo made the cover of Parade on February 1, 1976.

Take a Bow

When Paul Simon sought the Democratic nomination for President in 1988, he was dubbed the "anti-candidate." His small stature, large glasses and penchant for wearing bow ties gave him a bookish appearance, and his soft-spoken nature and self-effacing humor set him apart from the rest of the candidates. Although he did not win the party's nomination for the White House, Sen. Simon became a national figure and the bow tie became his trademark.

In 1996, Simon announced he would not seek reelection. As the Senate completed its business for the year, Simon arrived to cast his final vote and found the entire membership of the Senate decked out in bow ties in his honor.

Seeking Recognition

To many Americans, the identities of the leaders of Congress, even their own Representative, can be a mystery. In April, 2002, the Capitol Hill newspaper *Roll Call* surveyed tourists on the National Mall. Only 19 percent could name the Speaker of the House and fewer than half could name their own Representative in Congress.

This lack of recognition has resulted in some interesting encounters between Congressional leaders and the American public.

Howard Baker of Tennessee served 18 years in the Senate (1967-1985). In 1980, Baker ran for the Republican nomination for President. He held the post of Majority Leader of the Senate from 1981 to 1985, and was President Reagan's chief Republican ally in Congress. He later served as Reagan's Chief of Staff in the White House. Baker was a national figure, often turning up on TV news and talk shows.

Still, not everyone readily recognized the Senator from Tennessee. In a speech to the Senate in 1983, Baker related the following story:

"The other day I was walking from this Chamber back to my office, and an excited group stopped me and someone said, 'Say, I know who you are. Don't tell me. Let me guess. Let me remember. I'll get it in a minute.'

"I waited several seconds, and finally said, 'Howard Baker.'

"He said, 'No. That's not it.'"

A later Senate Majority Leader, Democrat Tom Daschle of South Dakota, told of an encounter he had with a constituent early in his political career.

On a cold winter day, Daschle was campaigning door-to-door. At one stop he was surprised when the woman who answered the door told him to wait while she got a check for him.

Daschle found himself thinking that campaigning wasn't so hard after all. His view changed when he looked at the check. It was made out to the Sioux Falls *Argus Leader,* the local newspaper.

Daschle recalled that, when he went back to the door, the woman said, "Well, I thought you were the paper boy."

In 2002, House Democratic Leader Richard Gephardt related an encounter he had. Gephardt said he was at the airport when two women approached him.

"Excuse us, but we've been looking at you and talking about you. And we know you're somebody," one of the ladies said to him. She asked him to settle a five-dollar bet they had made.

"I think you're Dan Quayle," she said, referring to the former Vice President. "My friend here thinks you do the weather on CNN."

THE BOW-TIED SENATOR

Sen. Paul Simon of Illinois turned the bow tie into his personal trademark.

PHOTO CREDIT:
U.S. Senate Historical Office

Camscam

In the early 1980's, a group of young Republicans in the House grew tired of their party's minority status in that body. They also rejected their leaders' gentlemanly practice of trying to get along with the Democratic majority. These rebellious young Republicans, led by Newt Gingrich of Georgia, Trent Lott of Mississippi, Jack Kemp of New York, Vin Weber of Minnesota and Robert Walker of Pennsylvania, instead adopted an in-your-face attitude and took every opportunity to attack Speaker Tip O'Neill and the Democrats in the House.

This group was handed a new weapon when TV cameras were installed in the House Chamber and C-SPAN initiated daily gavel-to-gavel coverage of the House proceedings. The coverage included Special Orders, a time at the end of the day when Members are freed from the restrictive rules of debate and may speak at length on any subject. They also took advantage of the fact that the TV cameras stayed tightly focused on the person speaking.

Night after night, the Republicans took to the lecterns to criticize O'Neill and other Democrats. They made impassioned pleas to their colleagues in the House, never letting on that they were speaking to an empty chamber.

Finally, on May 10, 1984, O'Neill had had enough. While the Republicans were attacking two dozen individual Democrats by name, O'Neill ordered the cameras to pan the empty room to show the speaker standing alone in the chamber.

Republicans cried foul, but O'Neill stuck to his position. Since then, the cameras regularly show the chamber during Special Orders, and a message is run along the bottom of the picture letting viewers know that the House has completed its legislative business for the day.

Despite "Camscam," as the incident became known, the attack politics worked for the Republicans. In the elections of 1994, the GOP took control of the House for the first time since the Eisenhower Administration and Gingrich was elected Speaker. Lott moved over to the Senate, and became Majority Leader of that body in 1996. Kemp served as Secretary of Housing and Urban Development in the cabinet of President George H.W. Bush, and ran for Vice President on the Republican ticket with Sen. Robert Dole in 1996.

As American as New Mexico

In 1986, Sens. Peter Domenici and Jeff Bingaman of New Mexico introduced a resolution in the Senate to bring recognition to their state. They weren't seeking recognition of their state's histor-

ical significance, natural beauty or cultural heritage. They just wanted New Mexico to be recognized as a state.

Domenici and Bingaman pointed out that many Americans confuse the state of New Mexico with the independent nation to our south, and introduced the resolution to call attention to this frequent error.

"For those who are not familiar with the geographic location of my State, the Land of Enchantment, it is directly south of Colorado, east of

HOUSE TV *(above)*

The proceedings of the House have been televised since 1979. The nonprofit network C-SPAN carries the feed provided by the House via cable and satellite to homes throughout the country.

PHOTO CREDIT:
House of Representatives

E PLURIBUS NEW MEXICO
(right)

The flag of New Mexico hangs with flags from the other 49 states along the tunnel connecting the Dirksen building with the Capitol, but some Americans still have a hard time recognizing the state as a part of the Union.

PHOTO CREDIT:
Jim Berard

Arizona, west of Texas, and north of the Mexican border," Domenici told the Senate. "I repeat, NORTH of the Mexican border. It was established as the 47th state in the Union in 1912."

Domenici said his state has "suffered an identity crisis at the hands of the federal government." He cited instances where New Mexico residents have seen interest payments on U.S. government bonds withheld because they were thought to be foreign nationals. He also said the State Department frequently referred inquiries from his office to the foreign desk.

"Grocery and drug stores in Washington have refused to honor New Mexico drivers' licenses, stating that it is their policy to take checks only from American citizens. When individuals are planning vacations in my beautiful state, there are frequent inquiries concerning visas, immunizations and the relative drinkability of our water. There are 1.3 million people who reside in the beautiful and sovereign State of New Mexico, fifth largest state in the Union, by area," Domenici said. "We use U.S. currency, not pesos."

Oh Yeah? Sez You!

During the 1988 Presidential campaign, the two candidates for Vice President squared off in a televised debate. Both candidates were sitting Senators, Republican Dan Quayle of Indiana and Democrat Lloyd Bentsen of Texas.

During the debate, Quayle was asked if, at age 41, he had the experience to hold an office that is a heartbeat away from the Presidency. Quayle likened his youthfulness to that of President John F. Kennedy, who was 43 when elected to the White House.

Bentsen, who was 67 at the time of the debate, had served with Kennedy in the House 40 years earlier. He bristled at the comparison, and responded to Quayle with the best zinger of the 1988 campaign: "I knew Jack Kennedy. Jack Ken-

nedy was a friend of mine. Senator, you're no Jack Kennedy."

Bentsen's reply made the highlights on the evening news, but did little good on Election Day. The Republican ticket of George H.W. Bush and Quayle trounced the Democratic team of Michael Dukakis and Bentsen.

In 2002, Sen. Robert Byrd of West Virginia took a page from his old colleague Bentsen's book when questioning Treasury Secretary Paul O'Neill about President George W. Bush's budget proposal. Byrd took offense at some passages in the budget document that criticized Congressional spending requests. As the debate with O'Neill heated, Byrd said, "With all respect to you, you are not Alexander Hamilton," referring to President Washington's Secretary of the Treasury.

Byrd, 84, did not claim to have known Hamilton personally.

Musical Chairs, Dakota Style

In 1992, Sen. Kent Conrad had a decision to make. The North Dakota Democrat was coming to the end of his first term, a term he won in an upset of incumbent Republican Mark Andrews. In that campaign, Conrad pledged he would fight to bring down the federal budget deficit, and promised not to run for a second term if he was not successful.

Six years later, a serious budget deficit still plagued the government, and Conrad decided to step down. Conrad's close friend, Rep. Byron Dorgan, immediately announced his candidacy for the open seat, and Conrad started looking for new work.

The deck shuffled on September 8 of that year, when the state's senior Senator, Quentin Burdick, died. Less populous states such as North Dakota rely on their Senators, and seniority is the key to influence in that body. North Dakotans knew they

THE DAKOTA DOUBLE

Sen. Kent Conrad of North Dakota is the only Senator in history to hold both seats from the same state on the same day.

PHOTO CREDIT:
Library of Congress.
Neg. no. LC-B18-1702

91

could not stand up to the larger states with two rookie Senators representing them. Democrats and Republicans alike approached Conrad and convinced him to reconsider his decision to retire.

After much soul searching, Conrad ran for and won Burdick's seat in a special election in December, a month after Dorgan was elected to the seat Conrad was vacating.

So, when the Senate reconvened in January and new Senators were sworn in, Conrad yielded the seat he had held for the past six years to Dorgan, and assumed the seat vacated by Burdick. In so doing he became the first Senator to hold both seats from the same state on the same day.

The Iron Man of the House

Rep. William Natcher of Kentucky was elected to the House in 1953. By the time of his death in 1994, the gentlemanly Democrat had set a record Cal Ripken Jr. would envy. In 41 years in the House of Representatives, Natcher cast 18,401 votes in a row.

In his later years, Natcher would carry small cards in his pocket, updated daily by his office, with the latest statistics on his voting record. He would hand out the cards to anyone inquiring about his streak.

It was not until he was terminally ill that Natcher's string came to an end, and only then after he was wheeled into the House Chamber on a hospital gurney for several votes.

Natcher was a throwback to an earlier, simpler era of public service. Although he lived in a time of spin doctors, massive campaign war chests and slick politicians on TV, Natcher operated with minimal staff. The soft-spoken Kentucky gentleman had no chief of staff or press secretary, choosing to handle those duties personally. The only money he would spend on his re-election campaigns was the filing fee he paid to get his name on the ballot.

THE TACTILE CAPITOL

In order to assist sight-impaired visitors to the Capitol complex, room numbers and other information signs are supplemented with Braille characters. Signs are also placed at uniform heights and locations relative to doors and other building features in order to make them easier to find and understand.

In addition, a tactile map of Capitol Hill and the National Mall with features in relief and labels in Braille, is located in the Capitol Crypt. Similar maps are located in the Hart building on the Senate side of the Capitol and the Rayburn building on the House side.

What Color Is Your Dog?

Over the years, many Southern politicians loyal to the Democratic Party described themselves as "Yellow Dog Democrats," based on the old saying "I'd vote for a yellow dog as long as he was a Democrat."

In the 1990's, a group of conservative House Democrats from various parts of the country formed a centrist coalition, but needed a catchy name. Partially inspired by the "yellow dog" slogan of the old Southern Democrats, and by a painting of a blue dog, they called themselves the Blue Dog Coalition.

New York's First Lady

On November 7, 2000, the voters of New York made history. They elected Hillary Rodham Clinton, wife of President Bill Clinton, to the United States Senate. The election marked the first time a First Lady had won elective office. In fact, since her Senate term and her husband's Presidential term overlapped by three weeks, Sen. Clinton served as both a U.S. Senator and First Lady for a short time.

Sen. Clinton's election also marked the first time a woman won statewide office in the state of New York.

Posthumous Politics, Part 2

On October 20, 2000, 28 years to the day after Reps. Boggs and Begich disappeared in a light plane crash in Alaska, Missouri Gov. Mel Carnahan was killed in a similar crash. Carnahan was running for the U.S. Senate at the time, trying to unseat incumbent John Ashcroft. Like Boggs and Begich, Carnahan was en route to a political event at the time of the crash. Unlike the victims in the earlier crash, Carnahan's fate was known immediately.

Carnahan's death put Missouri Democrats in a tough position. Before the crash, Carnahan and Ashcroft were running neck and neck in statewide polls, and the Democrats saw that they had a chance to unseat a Republican incumbent. With less than three weeks left until the election, there was no time to take Carnahan's name off the ballot, let alone find a replacement candidate and mount an effective campaign. Except...

Roger Wilson, Carnahan's Democratic successor as governor, had a plan. He announced that, if Mel Carnahan won the November election posthumously, he would appoint the late governor's widow, Jean Carnahan, to the seat.

When November 7 came and the votes were counted, Mel Carnahan won, Jean Carnahan stood ready to take her late husband's place in the U.S. Senate, and John Ashcroft became the first U.S. Senator to be unseated by a dead man.

The news wasn't all bad for Ashcroft, though. President-elect George W. Bush selected the Missouri Republican as his Attorney General. At his Senate confirmation hearing, he was introduced by his old Republican colleague from Missouri, Sen. Kit Bond, and the newly appointed junior Senator from the state, Jean Carnahan.

★ ★ ★

A DIVINELY INSPIRED GATE CRASHER

Even the tightest security net can have its holes.

On Inauguration Day, 2001, security at the Capitol was at its highest level. A new President and Vice President, George W. Bush and Richard Cheney, were to be sworn in. The ceremony would be attended by outgoing President Bill Clinton and Vice President Al Gore. The oath of office would be administered by Chief Justice William Rehnquist. The new President's father, former President George H.W. Bush, would be there, along with the leadership of both houses of Congress, the Supreme Court, the foreign diplomatic corps and scores of other dignitaries.

No one was to be allowed in the Capitol without the proper credentials, and those credentials were to be checked at several points to make sure no one slipped through.

That didn't deter the Rev. Richard C. "Rich" Weaver, a Christian minister from California. On that Inauguration Day, Weaver, who only had a standing room ticket at the back of the Capitol lawn for the ceremony, blended in with a group of VIP's, walked right into the Capitol and took a seat on the inaugural platform.

After the ceremony, an officer intercepted Weaver and directed him to an exit. When the

RADIOACTIVE STATUE

The statue of Roger Williams of Rhode Island showed the strongest readings in a study of radiation in the Capitol by the website Junkscience.com. However, the readings were not outside the limits of normal background radiation.

PHOTO CREDIT:
Jim Berard

minister stepped out the door, he found himself just a few feet away from the new President, who was getting ready to step into his limousine for the inaugural parade.

Weaver saw his opportunity. He calmly walked up to President Bush, shook his hand, wished him well, and presented him with a medallion and a card with an inspirational message. Weaver reached inside his jacket. He was going for a camera, but he decided that taking a picture at that point wouldn't have been appropriate.

In an interview with The Washington Post *about his exploit, Weaver credited God with his success at crashing the Inaugural. Weaver said he told the Secret Service agents who questioned him that his ability to slip through security had nothing to do with any lapse on their part. He said he told the officers, "God's bigger than all you guys."*

★ ★ ★

The Effect of Gamma Rays on Congress

Is the U.S. Capitol radioactive? A 2001 study of the Capitol and the Jefferson Building of the Library of Congress revealed up levels of gamma radiation up to 65 times higher than safety standards set by the U.S. Environmental Protection Agency.

The study, published by the website Junk Science.com, did not claim that visitors to the Capitol were at risk for exposure to the radiation. Instead, the purpose of the study was to lampoon a proposal by the EPA to set what the authors of the study deemed to be unrealistically stringent restrictions on material shipped to a nuclear waste repository in Yucca Mountain, Nevada.

The website called on Sen. Harry Reid of Nevada, a supporter of the EPA standards, to work as hard for the protection of visitors to the Capitol.

Just to be safe, the Architect of the Capitol dispatched a team to test radiation levels in the buildings. They detected the highest readings near marble or granite pedestals of statues, but found nothing stronger than normal background radiation.

★ ★ ★

THIRTY DAYS HATH NOVEMBER?

Each December the U.S. Capitol Historical Society publishes a calendar for the coming year. These calendars feature historical notes for each day of the year and each month features a beautiful photograph of a Washington landmark, such as the Lincoln Memorial, the White House or the Capitol.

The calendars, which retail for $5.95, are very popular and Members of Congress buy them to distribute to friends and key constituents.

When the 650,000 calendars for 2002 arrived from the printer, the Society noticed something strange. The month of November had 31 days.

New calendars were ordered, but the reprints did not arrive until March, seriously hurting sales.

★ ★ ★

The Old Man of the Senate

Strom Thurmond, the irrepressible politician from South Carolina, served in the U.S. Senate longer—48 years—than any other Senator.

Thurmond won election to his first term in the Senate in 1954. He did it by a write-in vote, the only Senator in history to win his seat in this fashion. Three years later, Thurmond delivered a speech that still holds the record as the longest in Senate history. He spoke for a full 24 hours and 18 minutes. In 1964, Thurmond switched his party affiliation from Democratic to Republican.

Thurmond continued to set records for longevity through 2002. This fact was not lost on his fellow Senator from South Carolina, Democrat Ernest Hollings, who often commented on his

own role as the most senior junior Senator in Congress. In November, 2001, Hollings chaired a meeting of a House-Senate conference committee on an aviation security bill. He opened by observing that the day marked the anniversary of his election to the Senate in 1966. "Here it is 35 years later and I'm still the junior Senator," an exasperated Hollings declared.

On December 5, 2001, Thurmond celebrated his 99th birthday. At a reception thrown by his fellow Senators, Thurmond, the oldest person to serve in the United States Senate, remarked, "I love you all. And, if you are a woman, I love you even more."

Much Ado about Lott

Thurmond's early career was characterized by his staunch support for segregation in the South, and the rights of Southern states to continue the tradition of separating their citizens according to race. In 1948, Thurmond ran for President as the nominee of the States Rights party, also known as the Dixiecrats, a splinter group made up of Southern Democrats who opposed their national party's support of civil rights.

As the years progressed, Thurmond gradually moved away from his segregationist views in favor of more mainstream conservative positions. As time went on, Thurmond's advanced age and growing frailty insulated him somewhat from criticism of his past politics. Thurmond's younger friend, Sen. Trent Lott of Mississippi, wasn't so lucky.

The end of Thurmond's service in the Senate coincided nicely with his 100th birthday in December, 2002. Friends and colleagues gathered to wish the senior Senator well at a combination birthday and retirement party. Lott, the Senate's Republican leader, was one of the featured speakers at the event. Lott was feeling good. His party had just retaken control of the Senate in the previous month's elections and Lott was poised to return as Majority Leader when Congress reconvened in a few weeks. However, the fates had different plans for Sen. Lott.

In his tribute to Thurmond, Lott spoke off the cuff and remarked that Mississippi had supported Thurmond's Dixiecrat ticket in the 1948 elections. He said his state was proud of that fact and opined that America would have had fewer problems had Thurmond been elected President that year.

Lott's remarks made national headlines. What was intended as a kindly tribute to a retiring colleague was seen by many as an endorsement of Thurmond's positions on race more than 50 years earlier. Lott explained. Lott apologized. Lott explained and apologized more, but he could not shake the criticism coming from Democrats and Republicans alike. He was forced to resign from his leadership position. It marked the first time scandal forced a party leader in the Senate to step down.

A Presidential Stepping Stone?

Twenty-seven Presidents served in Congress on their way to the White House and two served in Congress after their terms as President. But only a handful of Presidents came directly from the House or Senate.

RECORD HOLDER

Sen. Strom Thurmond of South Carolina is the only person to win election to the U.S. Senate by write-in vote. He holds the record for the longest speech in Senate history and served longer than any other Senator.

PHOTO CREDIT:
U.S. Senate

James Garfield is the only person to move directly from the House of Representatives to the White House. He was elected President in 1880. (Garfield had been elected to the Senate by the state legislature of Ohio for the term beginning in 1881, but was elected President before he had a chance to serve in the Senate.)

Only two incumbent Senators have won the nation's highest office: Warren G. Harding in 1920 and John F. Kennedy in 1960.

Fourteen Vice Presidents have eventually become President, but only 13 of them went directly from VP to Chief Executive. The exception was Richard Nixon, who spent eight years as a private citizen between his Vice Presidential and Presidential terms. Eight Vice Presidents ascended to the office because of the death of a President. Another, Gerald Ford, became President when his predecessor, Nixon, resigned. The only four sitting Vice Presidents to be elected President were John Adams (1796), Thomas Jefferson (1800), Martin Van Buren (1836) and George H. W. Bush (1988).

Or a Presidential Curse?

All three of the Presidents who came directly from the House or Senate—Garfield, Harding and Kennedy—died in office during their first term. Garfield was fatally shot after serving only four months as President. He languished two more months before he passed away and Vice President Chester A. Arthur became President.

Harding served just less than two years, five months before he died of an illness in 1923 and the Presidency was handed to VP Calvin Coolidge.

On November 22, 1963, Kennedy was shot and killed while on a Presidential visit to Dallas, just two years, 10 months into his Presidency. Later that day, Vice President Lyndon Johnson was sworn in as the 36th President of the United States.

Only in Washington

Earn money for just sitting on your behind? Or standing in one place? It happens nearly every day in Washington while Congress is in session.

With few exceptions, every meeting of every Congressional committee is open to the public free of charge. These meetings attract Congressional staff, reporters, activists, students, and tourists. They also attract lobbyists representing businesses and other organizations with an interest in the particular subject of the hearing. Most of the time there are plenty of seats to accommodate all spectators, but often, when the subject is controversial, or a major piece of legislation is being examined, or a high-profile witness is on the agenda, long lines can form outside the hearing rooms and seats may be hard to find. When a major tax bill is up for discussion, the line can form the night before.

In order to guarantee themselves a place in the room, many lobbying firms hire people to wait in line for them. They hire mostly students and day workers, usually through one of a handful of agencies in Washington that supply line sitters.

It's strictly a business proposition. It is a better use of resources to hire a line sitter to spend an hour or more at minimum wage than making a six-figure executive spend so much of his or her time waiting in line.

Standing Out in a Crowd

The dark suit is the preferred uniform for men serving in the Senate. In the House, a Congressman may don a sport jacket from time to time. Women in either chamber likewise tend to dress conservatively, although they will sometimes opt for brighter colors.

When the President visits the Capitol to deliver his annual State of the Union Address, the female Members of Congress are most likely to exercise their prerogative to wear bright suits and dresses. As the TV cameras pan the House chamber during the nationally televised speech, the women of Congress are easy to spot in their bright outfits of red, yellow and turquoise as they sit among a sea of men in dark suits.

A MAJOR LEAGUE MOVE?

Should the federal government move to another city, such as Charlotte or Memphis, if the new city promises to build it a new capitol?

A 2002 story in The Onion, *a journal of political satire, had Congress threatening to do just that. The tongue-in-cheek article quoted Speaker Dennis Hastert as expressing a nostalgic fondness for the old building, but complaining about the sightlines, bathrooms and lack of parking.*

The article even included a drawing of a new capitol with a retractable dome.

Of course, Congress had no intention of abandoning its current home. The article meant to spoof professional sports franchises, who frequently threaten to relocate unless their home cities build them better facilities.

That point was missed by news services in China, who ran the story as a legitimate news item.

The Sanchez Sisters

The 2002 elections brought Congress its first sister act. Linda Sanchez, newly elected Representative from Los Angeles, joined her older sister, Loretta Sanchez, a four-term Congresswoman from Orange County, California. It marked the first time a pair of sisters has served together in either the House or Senate.

FRENCH FREE

During World War I, many Americans showed their displeasure with Germany by renaming sauerkraut "liberty cabbage." Nearly a century later, food again became an instrument of foreign policy.

In early 2003, the United States was preparing to take military action against Iraq. Our long-time ally, France, opposed the war, and that stirred up some American resentment against the French.

Several Members of Congress made speeches critical of the French government for its position on the war. Some went so far as to call upon Americans to boycott French products.

Reps. Bob Ney of Ohio and Walter Jones of North Carolina went even farther. Acting on a suggestion offered by Jones, Ney, the Chairman of the House Administration Committee, directed the House restaurants to stop serving French fries. Instead, the House eateries would offer "Freedom fries."

Ney and Jones didn't forget breakfast, either. "Freedom toast" soon occupied the spot on the menu formerly held by French toast.

Like Father Like Daughter

In 2002, after 22 years in the Senate, Frank Murkowski of Alaska resigned to serve as his state's governor. As governor, he had the duty to appoint his successor in the Senate. Murkowski chose his daughter, and Lisa Murkowski became the first daughter to follow her father into the U.S. Senate.

The first daughter to succeed her father in Congress preceded Lisa Murkowski's appointment by some 80 years. In 1922, Winifred Mason Huck of Illinois won a special election to fill out the unexpired term of her deceased father, Rep. William E. Mason. She served for only four months and failed to win the nomination to run for a full term.

7
GHOSTS!

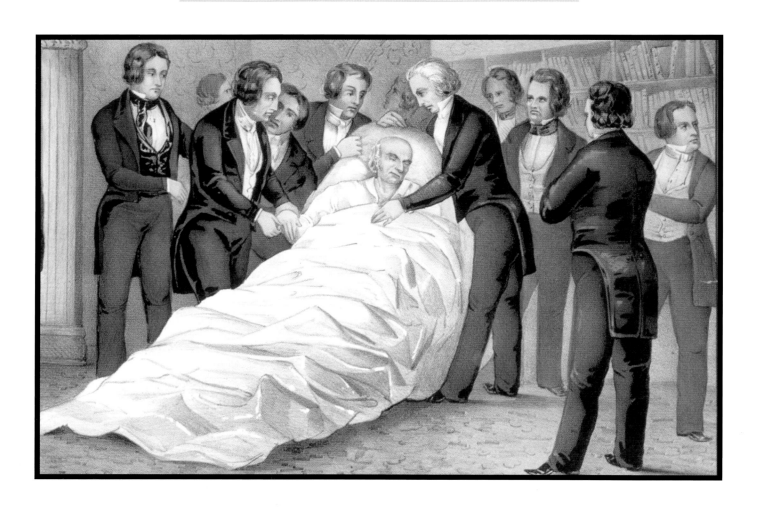

The U.S. Capitol is said to be one of the most haunted places in Washington, D.C.

It is one of the oldest buildings in the city, so it has had more opportunity to collect spirits than most of the other structures in town. It is also full of obscure rooms, labyrinthine corridors and hidden stairwells.

At night, when the politicians and tourists are gone, it can be a lonely place. Its hard stone walls produce eerie echoes. The mighty iron dome groans as it cools in the night air, and, when the light is just right, its statues, pillars and curtains can cast scary shadows.

This chapter relates a number of stories of ghostly sights and sounds reported in the Capitol by guards, cleaners and others who have wandered its empty halls in the quiet of the night. Are they true? Who can tell for sure? A 1935 article in *The Washington Post* noted that ghost sightings in the Capitol dropped off during the Prohibition years, only to pick up again after repeal.

Are these stories the product of too much drink, a bad meal or other ingestions? Or are they to be believed? You be the judge.

The Curse

Spooky happenings at the Capitol may be the result of a curse placed on it by one of its builders.

In 1808, when the Capitol was under construction, architect B. Henry Latrobe disagreed with construction superintendent John Lenthall over the vaulting in the room now known as the Old Supreme Court Chamber. Lenthall had the vaulting done his way.

When Lenthall and his men began to remove the braces from his vaults, they heard an ominous crack. Workmen scattered, running and jumping out doors, windows, any available exit. The falling masonry from the collapsing ceiling landed on Lenthall and fatally crushed him.

Legend has it that, with his dying breath, the unfortunate builder—and loser of the argument—placed a curse on the building, which may explain many of the ghostly sightings chronicled here, as well as some actions of Congress.

By the way, the vaulting you now see in the chamber is Latrobe's design.

The Demon Cat

The Capitol's most famous and frightening ghost is that of a black cat that roams the corridors at night.

The Demon Cat, as the creature is called, has been seen many times. Perhaps the spirit of a cat once brought into the building to control the mouse population, the Demon Cat is the only Capitol ghost held responsible for the death of one of its witnesses.

The cat is most often found in the lowest reaches of the building, in the area where a tomb was constructed for George and Martha Washington, but it has haunted other parts of the Capitol as well.

When the Demon Cat is first spotted, it appears to be just an ordinary black house cat. As it gets closer, the cat grows ever bigger and more menacing, until it reaches gigantic proportions—10 feet high and 10 feet wide, according to one report. Then, the cat vanishes like a burst bubble. It is said one aging guard was so frightened by the sight of the feline phantom that he suffered a heart attack and died a short time later.

At least one guard has fired his gun at the ghostly cat, to no apparent effect.

Some accounts of the Demon Cat link its appearance to the advent of major changes or crises in the country. Others say the cat appears when visitors attempt to deface the Capitol walls with graffiti or other vandalism.

(opposite page)

THE DEATH OF "OLD MAN ELOQUENT"

John Quincy Adams suffered a stroke on the floor of the old hall of the House of Representatives and died hours later in the adjacent Speaker's office. Some say his spirit still haunts Statuary Hall.

PHOTO CREDIT:
Library of Congress
Neg. no. LC-USZC4-5802

Are these ghostly cat stories mere legends? Are they the products of the overactive minds of bored night watchmen, or even hallucinations? Hard to say. But the Capitol does hold one shred of physical evidence of a cat's visit. It can be found on the first floor of the Senate wing, outside the Old Supreme Court Chamber, near the lower portion of the Small Senate Rotunda. Clearly visible at the base of a stone pillar are five tiny cat's pawprints, coming from nowhere, leading to nowhere, eternally imbedded in the solid stone floor.

The General

John A. Logan, a Democrat from Illinois, served in the House of Representatives from 1859 until 1862, when he resigned to accept a commission in the Union army during the Civil War. Logan rose to the rank of Major General by the war's end. His military record won him the honor of a statue in Northwest Washington, in a spot aptly named Logan Circle.

Back in civilian life, Logan returned to politics and was reelected to the House, this time as a Republican, and was one of the managers of the resolution impeaching President Andrew Johnson. In 1871, he was elected to the U.S. Senate, and served until 1886, with a slight detour in 1884 when he ran unsuccessfully for Vice President of the United States. During Logan's last four years in the Senate, he served as chairman of the Committee on Military Affairs and the Militia (later renamed the Committee on Armed Services).

Logan died on December 26, 1886, but his spirit may still haunt the Capitol.

Night guards walking near the room in the Senate wing where Logan's committee used to meet often have reported an eerie sight. At precisely 12:30 a.m., the door to the hearing room would quietly open and, a few seconds later, out would step the specter of the old general himself, surrounded by a blue haze.

After about 15 seconds, the apparition would step back into the committee room and quietly close the door behind him.

THE GENERAL'S HORSE

Workers installing a new air conditioning system in the Capitol in the 1930's came upon an unusual discovery: a stuffed horse.

According to a Washington Post *article of January 2, 1938, workers had drilled a hole in an office wall to run electrical lines. They pushed the wire into the hole, but it didn't come out where they expected. They then removed part of the wall to see what was behind it.*

The wall, it turned out, covered a door to a sealed-up room. One of the workers told the Post no one wanted to open the door, for fear of falling victim to a curse such as the one that befell the discoverers of King Tut's tomb. After a few minutes, though, overcome by reason, curiosity and a sense of duty, they opened the mysterious door and found the horse inside the hidden room.

One of the workmen insisted that the horse belonged to Gen. Logan, because it looked just like the one the General rides in his statue in Logan Circle.

"Of course the coat was a little dusty and dull-looking, but there was the same proud tilt of the head," the workman told the paper.

He said the General's ghost won't have to walk the halls of the Capitol any more, because now he has his horse.

Ghostly Footsteps

The room now known as Statuary Hall served as the House of Representatives chamber from 1807 until 1857. The walls of the room are lined with bronze and marble statues of the famous and the obscure, sent to Washington by their home states to hold a place of honor in the Capitol.

Former President John Quincy Adams died in a room adjacent to this chamber on February 23, 1848.

Capitol Police making their rounds often speak of hearing ghostly footsteps follow behind them as they walk across the stark black-and-white tile floor. The sounds keep pace with the officer's own footsteps.

Could these sounds be the steps of John Quincy Adams, following the visitor across the floor of the chamber where he worked and died? Or are they simply echoes of the walker's own footfalls, generated by the strange acoustics of the hall?

One officer was determined to find out. He wore rubber-soled shoes to work one night. In the quiet of the early morning, he made his usual pass through Statuary Hall. As his rubber-clad feet trod silently across the floor, he heard the distinct sound of footsteps behind him, walking when he walked, stopping when he stopped.

The guard suspected a prankster, a co-worker hiding among the statues, perhaps. So he led the trailing footsteps into a corner, hoping to trap his tormentor. When he spun around to confront the jokester, there was no one there.

Congress in Session

Statuary Hall is the site of other ghostly happenings as well. A guard is said to have seen the 1848 House of Representatives, John Quincy Adams included, in session there one night.

One report of the incident said the guard was a student working his way through college as a night watchman. His American history class was studying the 1848 era at the time of his vision, so the young guard may have simply fallen asleep while studying on watch and dreamed of the apparition.

Another report said the guard was subsequently fired for drunkenness.

The Two Librarians

For the first 100 years or so of its history, the Capitol housed the Library of Congress. At least two of the building's ghosts relate to that time. One of the ghosts is that of a Mr. Twine. It was Mr. Twine's job to stamp the government's identification mark on new books in the library's collection. In order to protect the valuable new volumes, Mr. Twine worked in a cage-like room fashioned from iron bars in the Capitol's basement. Hour after hour, day after day, Mr. Twine stamped the books with a solution of lampblack and alcohol. All day long, the sound of stamp, stamp, stamp was heard from Mr. Twine's cage.

Now, a century later, guards patrolling the Capitol basement can sometimes hear Mr. Twine still at work: Stamp. Stamp. Stamp.

A library colleague of Mr. Twine is also said to haunt the Capitol's cellar. His name is lost to history and he is known simply as the Old Cataloguer.

This man also worked for many years in a restricted area of the basement, cataloguing the Library's massive collections. One day, the Old Cataloguer suffered a stroke and was incapacitated. Unable to speak, he excitedly gestured to his

THE GENERAL

General James Logan's statue stands in Logan Circle in Northwest Washington, D.C. Does the General's ghost haunt the Capitol? And what about his horse?

PHOTO CREDIT:
Jim Berard

care givers that he wanted to go to the vault where he did his work. His doctors said no, and the cataloguer died soon after.

Library officials later discovered, stuffed into some of the dusty volumes the Old Cataloguer's vault, some $6,000 in currency and uncashed money orders (or government bonds, according to some reports).

It is said the Old Cataloguer still wanders the Capitol basement, searching for his lost money.

Keystone Boss

Boies Penrose, a Pennsylvania Republican, served in the Senate from 1897 until his death in 1921. As chairman of the powerful Finance Committee, he was known as "Keystone Boss."

Penrose was a large man, an imposing figure who filled his chair "the way a muffin fills a muffin tin," according to one description. A bachelor with no children, Penrose kept a room at the Wardman Park Hotel, with only a servant for companionship. Since the Senator had no reason to hurry home to his lonely hotel room at the end of the workday, he would spend the early evening sitting in the Finance Committee's hearing room, gazing out at the Mall and the setting sun, lost in his meditations.

When Penrose died on December 31, 1921, the bell in the Finance Committee room rang loudly and long, announcing his death, although some say it was just a premature celebration of the New Year. A 1935 newspaper article reported that Senate pages still heard the bell ring out at odd times from that room, but that is not the only ghostly phenomenon following Penrose's death.

Some visitors to the hearing room at night believe the Senator still haunts the room where he spent so many hours in solitude. One page told of going into the room in search of a book. Because he could not find the light switch—which was located in an odd place near the floor—the page groped around in the dark for what he wanted. As he did, he suddenly saw the imposing figure of Keystone Boss Penrose sitting at the committee table, silently staring at him. The page left the room in a panic, without the book.

The Killer Bathtub

In the mid- to late-1800's, the Senate installed a bathhouse for its members in the basement of the Senate wing. Appointed with two marble tubs imported from Italy, polished tile and a crystal chandelier, the spa became a popular spot for weary Senators to take a soak and relax after a stressful day.

One of those who especially enjoyed "tubbing," as the practice was called, was Henry Wilson, Vice President under Ulysses S. Grant. On November 22, 1875, Wilson was soaking in one of the marble tubs. The warm bath relaxed him so well that he drifted off to sleep. As he slept, his bath water cooled.

When he awoke, the Vice President found himself shivering naked in a tub full of cold water. Although the bath had only cooled to room temperature, to Wilson it felt like ice water.

Chilled to the bone, Wilson made it back to his office near the Senate Chamber, but it was too late. The chill triggered a stroke and Wilson died in his office that night.

Since Wilson's death, people passing by his old office often hear mysterious sneezes, even though there is no one in the room. There have also been reports of feeling a damp chill in the doorway to the room and catching a faint whiff of scented soap, the kind they used in the Senate bath in 1875.

THE BOSS

Sen. Boies Penrose of Pennsylvania spent so much time in his Finance Committee office that some believe he may have never left.

PHOTO CREDIT:
Library of Congress
Neg. no. LC-usz62-109681

The Bloody Steps

A narrow marble stairway leading from the Congressional dining room on the first floor to the House Chamber on the second floor bears the evidence of a violent episode in the Capitol's history, and may hold even more than that.

On February 28, 1890, a former two-term Democratic Congressman from Kentucky named William Taulbee encountered journalist Charles Kincaid on this stairway. The two argued over stories Kincaid had written about Taulbee. As the argument grew more heated, Kincaid pulled a gun and shot the ex-Congressman, fatally wounding him. Taulbee died two weeks later at a nearby hospital.

Taulbee's blood still stains the marble steps. Although they have tried many times, cleaners have not been able to cleanse the now blackened bloodstains out of the porous stone.

It is believed that Taulbee's spirit also remains on the stairway, taking his revenge by tripping reporters who use the marble steps.

THE GHOST WHO WASN'T

When a Senator dies in office, his family can request that the funeral services be held in the Senate chamber. Such was the case of Sen. Isham G. Harris of Tennessee, who died on July 8, 1897.

Elected Governor of Tennessee in 1857, Harris brought his state into the Confederacy, and fought for the South during the Civil War. He fled to Mexico, then England after the war, but returned to Memphis to resume his law practice. He was elected to the U.S. Senate in 1877 and served there for 20 years.

During the Senator's later years in office, an engineer named Jones worked in the Capitol building. Jones worked the night shift and was known to stroll around the building in his stocking feet. Jones was also said to bear a strong resemblance to Harris.

On the night before Harris' funeral, a guard was posted in the Senate Chamber to keep watch over the casket. The tired, bored watchman dozed off briefly, but when he awoke, he saw the figure of the dead Senator from Tennessee standing beside the coffin.

The watchman let out a scream that was heard more than a block away as he bolted from the Senate chamber.

About an hour later, when colleagues were able to settle him down, the frightened guard learned the truth. He hadn't seen the dead Senator's ghost at all. It was just Jones, stopping by the chamber to pay his last respects to his late look-alike.

BATHTUB VICTIM
(left)

Vice President Henry Wilson caught a chill in a Senate bath and died in his office near the Senate chamber. Some say his ghost still haunts the room.

PHOTO CREDIT:
Library of Congress
Neg. no. LC-USZ62-96499

SCENE OF THE CRIME

Blood still stains the marble steps in the House wing where former Rep. William Taulbee was fatally shot in 1890.

PHOTO CREDIT:
Jeff Lesnik

The Unlucky Stonemason

According to legend, a stonemason working on the early construction of the Capitol was sealed inside one of the building's marble walls. Some tellings claim it was an accident, other say it was the result of a fight with another worker. (In reality, this story may be a corruption of the accident that killed builder John Lenthall in the Old Supreme Court Chamber in 1808.)

Still, witnesses have reported seeing the figure of a workman, trowel in hand, walking in the Capitol, then disappearing from sight into a solid stone wall. Others have reported the sound of the scraping of the mason's trowel.

The Ghostly Assassin

The figure of Charles Guiteau, assassin of President James Garfield, is another specter said to roam the Capitol halls.

On July 2, 1881, Guiteau, a disgruntled office-seeker, shot Garfield at the old Baltimore and Potomac Railroad station, just a few blocks from the Capitol.

Garfield died September 11, after only six months in office. His body was placed in the Capitol Rotunda to lie in state. Guiteau was tried, convicted and hanged for the assassination.

President Garfield's ghost has also been reported in the Capitol, perhaps wondering what he might have accomplished if his time in office had not been cut so short.

Spiritual Tunes

"Bishop" Simms was the name of a man who once worked in the Senate barbershop. He was called Bishop because he purported to be a part-time preacher, but his religious affiliation was not clear.

Simms possessed a wonderful singing voice, and would often sing as he worked. His music charmed those who heard it and provided a respite from the political debates that usually raged around the shop.

Many years after his death, people still reported hearing the mellow voice of Bishop Simms in and around the barbershop.

Party Time!

Some of the Capitol's night workers have told of an unusual occurrence in Statuary Hall. When the hour is late and the mood is right, the bronze and marble statues in the hall come to life and throw themselves a party. One guard said he saw Civil War adversaries Ulysses S. Grant and Robert E. Lee dismount their pedestals and meet for a friendly handshake.

One version of this story says the statues party on the night a new President is sworn in, throwing their own inaugural ball in Statuary Hall.

While the statues in the Capitol probably have a fine time at these midnight soirees, dancing must be a problem. There are only six statues of women in the National Statuary Hall Collection, while there are 91 statues honoring men. Even if you eliminate the four Catholic priests and one Puritan from the count, it still leaves more than 14 male dance partners for each of the ladies.

No wonder the statue of Florence Sabin shows her sitting down. She's probably resting her tired feet.

Daniel Webster's Wine Cellar

In 1987, Sen. Patrick Leahy of Vermont took possession of a new Capitol "hideaway." The room, he was told, was once a storeroom where Daniel Webster kept his private wine supply, and the ghost of Webster had been known to visit there. Shortly after moving in, Leahy decided to make peace with the famed 19th Century orator, and named his new office the Daniel Webster Room.

He also set aside an invitation for Webster to the room's dedication, in case the old Senator's ghost wanted to pay a visit to his old haunt.

Ghost in the Wiring?

The ghosts of the Capitol complex may not be confined to the Capitol itself. In 1991, Rep. Bill Orton of Utah and his staff noticed some unusual activity in their office suite in the Longworth House Office Building. Lights flickered and bells sounded without reason or explanation. Rep. Susan Molinari of New York told the *Detroit News* that, when she occupied the suite, she and her staff occasionally found doors to empty rooms locked from the inside.

The problems with the lights and bells were blamed on bad wiring, and ceased to occur when new wiring was installed.

Other Ghosts

Other ghostly sights and sounds in the Capitol:

—The ghost of Pierre L'Enfant, who designed the capital city for the new federal government. Fired from his job without being paid, L'Enfant died in poverty.

—A Revolutionary War soldier, standing guard near the tomb designed for George Washington.

—A cleaner who died on the job. On quiet nights, the slosh of his pail and scrub of his brush on the marble and tile floors can still be heard.

—A "gaunt specter" said to haunt the Senate dining room.

—A well-dressed gentleman with a dark mustache, usually seen on the lower floors of the House wing, walking with his hands clasped behind him. His appearance gives him the look of a foreigner, possibly a diplomat.

—A World War I soldier, who appears when a body lies in the Rotunda. The soldier materializes just long enough to snap to attention and salute the dead honoree, then vanishes. It may be the spirit of the Unknown Soldier from World War I, whose flag-draped casket lay in the Rotunda in 1921 en route to Arlington National Cemetery.

SITTING ONE OUT

As one of the few women represented in Statuary Hall, Florence Sabin is probably a popular dance partner for the overwhemingly male collection.

PHOTO CREDIT:
Jim Berard

8

CANINGS, GUNFIGHTS AND FISTICUFFS

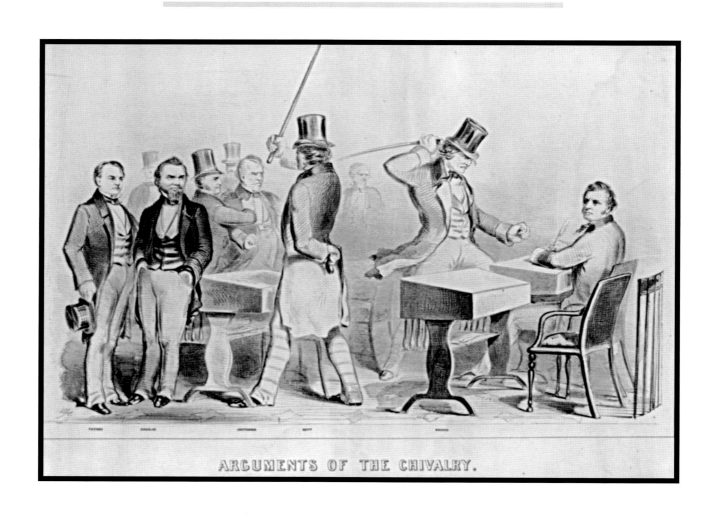

ARGUMENTS OF THE CHIVALRY.

Danger is no stranger to the U.S. Capitol. From the founding of the nation, political arguments have escalated into fistfights or worse, sometimes with tragic results. In the early 19th Century, Senators and Representatives often carried pistols to work in order to protect themselves from their fellow legislators. Blood still stains the House wing stairway where a reporter fatally shot a former Congressman during an argument in 1890. And fistfights still occasionally break out among disagreeing Congressmen when the hour gets late and tempers get short.

This chapter looks at some of the duels, fistfights and other such events that have involved Members of Congress.

In 1798, two years before Congress moved to the new Capitol, Rep. Roger Griswold of Connecticut attacked Rep. Matthew Lyon of Vermont with a "stout hickory stick." Lyon fended off the attack with a set of fireplace tongs. The two men wrestled to the floor before other Members broke up the fight. Neither was hurt.

The confrontation began two weeks earlier when Griswold accused Lyon of cowardice during the Revolutionary War, and Lyon responded by spitting tobacco juice in Griswold's face.

Vice President Aaron Burr shot and killed former Treasury Secretary Alexander Hamilton on July 11, 1804, in a duel at Weehauken, N.J., after their political rivalry degenerated into a personal feud. Burr escaped murder charges and resumed his duties as Vice President.

Armistead Thomson Mason had a promising life ahead of himself, except he was a hothead who would demand satisfaction on the dueling grounds for every perceived insult or slight. At age 25 he achieved the rank of colonel of the Virginia Volunteers during the War of 1812. He later served as a brigadier general in the Virginia Mi-

litia. Mason was elected to the Senate in 1816 to fill out the final year of the term vacated by the resignation of William B. Giles.

In the fall of 1816, Mason ran for a full term, and lost. The bitter campaign was characterized by several duels. In 1819, Mason fought a duel with his brother-in-law, John Mason McCarty, at the dueling grounds at Bladensburg, Maryland. Mason lost.

In 1826, Secretary of State Henry Clay, who swung the election of 1824 to John Quincy Adams, and Sen. John Randolph of Virginia, a staunch supporter of Adams' rival, Andrew Jackson, faced off in a duel with pistols. Both survived.

Rep. Jonathan Cilley of Maine was fatally wounded in a duel with Rep. William Graves of Kentucky in 1839. The two men had fought with rifles. Cilley became the only sitting Member of the House to die in a duel. His death prompted Congress to ban dueling—even issuing or accepting a challenge to duel—within the limits of the District of Columbia.

As the Civil War approached, debate over issues affecting slavery, especially whether slavery would be permitted in new states coming into the Union, heated to the boiling point. Fights erupted in the Senate over Henry Clay's proposed Compromise of 1850.

Sen. Thomas Hart Benton of Missouri supported the compromise, even though he came from a slave state. This branded him a traitor to the Southern cause in the eyes of Sen. Henry "Hangman" Foote of Mississippi, who pulled a loaded pistol on Benton. Benton, in turn, taunted Foote by opening his shirt, baring his chest and daring Foote to fire at an unarmed man. Foote was disarmed before he could take Benton's dare.

Rep. Preston Brooks of South Carolina took exception to remarks Sen. Charles Sumner of Massachusetts had made about Brooks' uncle, South Carolina Sen. A.P. Butler. On May 22, 1856, Brooks and fellow South Carolinian, Rep. Lawrence M. Keitt, charged into the Senate Chamber. They found Sumner writing at his desk.

Sen. Thomas Hart Benton and Harry "Hangman" Foote square off in the Senate Chamber

SCENE IN UNCLE SAM'S SENATE.

"GO AHEAD AND SHOOT"

Sen. Thomas Hart Benton of Missouri taunts Sen. Henry "Hangman" Foote of Mississippi by baring his chest as Foote points a pistol at the unarmed Benton in an 1850 lithograph.

PHOTO CREDIT:
Library of Congress
Neg. no. LC-USZ62-4835

With Keitt holding off the other Senators, Brooks proceeded to strike Sumner fiercely with a cane, beating the Massachusetts Senator to the floor and leaving him in a bloody heap. Sumner was carried from the chamber and did not return to the Senate for more than three years. Brooks and Keitt were not disciplined by the House, since many of their fellow Southerners considered them heroes for beating down the antislavery Senator.

Keitt was at the center of another Congressional tussle in 1858, this time in the House. During an especially hot debate, Keitt hurled insults at Rep. Galusha Grow of Pennsylvania. Grow lunged at Keitt and other Members joined the fight.

The fracas ended on a comic note when one Congressman managed to snatch the hairpiece off another's head, waved it in the air and declared, "I've got his scalp!

In 1859, Rep. Dan Sickles of New York chased down and fatally shot his wife's lover, Philip Barton Key. Sickles was the first person in American history to successfully use the insanity defense in a murder case.

Also in 1859, Sen. David Broderick, a Democrat from California, was mortally wounded in a duel with the Chief Justice of the California Supreme Court. Broderick remains the only sitting Senator to die in a duel.

Although he served as a Senator from California, Broderick was born in Washington, D.C. His father, an immigrant stonecutter from Ireland, came to Washington to work on the Capitol.

★ ★ ★

SNUFF'S ENOUGH

Not every disagreement between Members of Congress was destined to end in a duel.

In 1841, Sen. William King, a Democrat from Alabama, and Henry Clay, leader of the majority Whig party in the Senate, argued over the assignment of the printing contract for the Senate. Clay wanted the contract withdrawn from the current vendor, a local Democratic-leaning newspaper publisher. King defended the publisher and exchanged strong words with Clay. The argument culminated in King issuing a written challenge to Clay.

Dueling was illegal in Washington by this time. So was issuing or accepting a challenge. The Sergeant at Arms of the Senate and a local court intervened and prevented the challenge from going any further.

Instead, Clay and King issued formal apologies to each other on the floor of the Senate. Clay sealed the peace by walking over to King's desk and asking for a pinch of snuff.

The two shook hands and bloodshed was avoided.

Representatives in the Ring?

By 1927, fistfights were so common on the floor of the House that Rep. James Gallivan of Massachusetts introduced a resolution to allow Members of Congress to settle their personal differences in the boxing ring.

Gallivan's resolution called upon the Speaker to set up a Boxing Board to regulate the bouts and rank Members according to weight, age and experience. It named Rep. William Upshaw of Georgia to referee the fights and called for the bouts to be held in Statuary Hall "under the paternal eye of the Fathers of the Republic."

Police Protection?

The primary mission of the U.S. Capitol Police is to ensure the safety of Members of Congress. That was not the way one Member was treated in an incident in July, 1947.

The freshman Representative was in dire need of a telephone. He went to a guard's station and asked to use the phone there. Not recognizing the rookie Congressman, the officer at the desk refused his request. When the Member insisted and reached for the phone, the policeman pulled his billy club on the startled politician.

The officer involved was fired from the force, but his name and the identity of the Congressman were not made public. Newspaper accounts also did not report if the Member ever got to make his phone call.

DUELING GROUND

A roadside marker in Arlington, Virginia, identifies the location where Henry Clay and John Randolph of Roanoke fought their famous duel.

PHOTO CREDIT:
Jim Berard

9

"A FIRETRAP"

BRITISH BURN THE CAPITOL · 1814

Since the Capitol's early days, fire has been a constant threat. For its first 100 years, the Capitol housed Congress, the Supreme Court, the Library of Congress and was the repository for most public records. By the end of the 19th Century, books and documents were stored in every available musky basement nook and musty attic cranny in the Capitol, creating a serious fire hazard.

The Court and the Library have since moved to their own quarters, and the creation of the National Archives and Records Administration has provided a safe repository for federal documents. The threat of fire has lessened, but not disappeared. In 1961, Rep. Frank T. Bow of Ohio said the building "could go up in almost an hour." A 1998 Washington Post article called the building "a firetrap."

The Architect of the Capitol is constantly working to upgrade the Capitol complex's fire resistance. Sprinklers and smoke detectors have been installed. Wiring has been upgraded, storage areas cleared, and evacuation procedures tested. Still, fire remains a constant concern.

The Attack of the Redcoats

The worst disaster to befall the Capitol took place before the building was even completed.

On August 24, 1814, during the War of 1812, British forces under the command of Admiral Sir George Cockburn marched on Washington.

The veteran British troops brushed past a defense force made up mostly of local militia, led by President James Madison, at the Maryland suburb of Bladensburg. Washington lay open and defenseless to the invaders.

Once in the city, Cockburn's men set fire to the new capital's public buildings. At the White House, Cockburn and his officers feasted on a dinner set out by First Lady Dolley Madison for the American defenders of the city. Mrs. Madison and the White House staff had evacuated just ahead of Cockburn's arrival. After dinner, the British put the White House to the torch.

At the Capitol, Cockburn is said to have stood atop the Speaker's chair in the House of Representatives chamber and asked his men, "Shall this harbor of Yankee democracy be burned?"

His troops answered with a rousing "Aye!"

Using the chairs and desks of Congressmen and Senators and the books of the fledgling Library of Congress for fuel, the British soldiers set fire to the Capitol.

Cockburn's wrath was not limited to government buildings. He saved some of his ire for the Washington press corps. He sent his men to silence the presses at the *National Intelligencer*, a paper that had criticized Cockburn's earlier actions against the United States in the war. He further ordered the destruction of all the letters C in the paper's fonts, "so that the rascals can no longer abuse my name."

Only a sudden rainstorm kept the fires from spreading to homes and businesses throughout the city. By the time the flames were put out, the Capitol was a charred, empty shell.

Despite the devastation to Washington, the British again failed to subdue American independence. Two weeks after the burning of the capital, the British fleet was turned back at Ft. McHenry in Baltimore Harbor. That battle inspired the poem that became our National Anthem. A few months later, the war was over.

In 1815, after the defeat of Napoleon at the Battle of Waterloo, Adm. Cockburn escorted the deposed French emperor to exile on the British island of St. Helena, and remained on the island as its governor for another year. It is said that Cockburn took pity on Napoleon and prevented his sailors from ceremoniously dunking the Little Corporal in the ocean when their ship crossed the Equator.

(opposite page)

BRITISH ATTACK

A painting by Allyn Cox on the ceiling of a first-floor corridor in the House wing shows British troops burning the unfinished Capitol in 1814.

PHOTO CREDIT:
Jim Berard

ANOTHER COCKBURN
INVADES WASHINGTON

More than a century after Adm. Cockburn's British forces sacked and burned the Capitol, Claud Cockburn, a descendant "by cousinly marriage" of the Admiral, was sent to Washington as a correspondent for The Times *of London. Ironically, he arrived as a fire burned at the Capitol.*

"On the black night of January 3, 1930, I saw the dome of the United States Capitol aflame," Claud Cockburn wrote. "Arriving five minutes earlier at Union Station, I was the first member of my family to set foot in Washington in a little more than 115 years. The last one before me burned the Capitol down."

The fire Claud Cockburn saw was ignited by a stray cigarette. It was confined to an attic room near the dome and caused only minor damage.

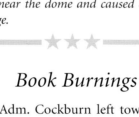

Book Burnings

After Adm. Cockburn left town, no fire at the Capitol has come anywhere near to the spectacle and destruction of the 1814 blaze, but two fires in the Library of Congress alerted officials to the constant danger fire posed to the building.

In 1826, a candle left burning when the library closed for the night started a fire that caused $3,000 damage. The fire prompted the House Committee on the Library to look into ways to fireproof the two-year-old library. The committee concluded that there was no practical way to do it.

Instead, Congress asked architect Charles Bulfinch to help reduce the threat of fire in the building overall. Bulfinch recommended the construction of a terrace on the West Front of the Capitol. The terrace, set a safe distance away from the building, would contain storage areas for coal and firewood and would also improve the view of the Capitol from the west.

Despite these efforts, fire returned to the library on Christmas Eve, 1851. A defective chimney flue set fire to one of the library's alcoves. A guard noticed the fire in its early stages, and could have put out the flames himself before much damage was done, but there was no water supply nearby. By the time he returned with water, the fire had spread. Firefighters and U.S. Marines battled the flames. A wooden rooftop staircase leading up to the dome had to be ripped down before the fire could climb it and set the wooden dome ablaze.

Bulfinch's magnificent library was burned out to the walls. The fire destroyed 35,000 volumes. About two-thirds of Thomas Jefferson's personal collection was lost, along with Gilbert Stuart portraits of the first five Presidents and other priceless works of art.

Architect Thomas U. Walter was commissioned to rebuild the library space. He designed a fireproof room of cast-iron, decorated with gold and bronze.

Walter's impressive work on the library and the wooden dome's susceptibility to fire helped sell Congress on the need for a new, fireproof, cast-iron dome for the Capitol.

Gas Attack

An explosion beneath the small Senate rotunda outside the Old Supreme Court Chamber rocked the Capitol on November 6, 1898. At first, some believed the blast was the work of Spanish saboteurs, since the Spanish-American War had just concluded. An investigation, however, traced the source to a faulty gas meter in the Capitol's basement.

The explosion heavily damaged the law library, the room now known as the Old Supreme Court Chamber, and the Small Senate Rotunda outside

**LEADING
THE INVASION**

Admiral Sir George Cockburn led the British invasion of Washington.

PHOTO CREDIT:
Library of Congress
Neg. no. LC-USZ62-12334

the chamber. Windows were broken and doors were blown out throughout the old Senate wing of the building.

Like the earlier fires in the Library of Congress, the explosion alerted the Architect of the Capitol and Congress to the danger fire posed, especially in the older sections of the building, where wood was used extensively in the framing and roof. In 1901, workers removed the wooden roofs over the old north and south wings and west center section of the Capitol and replaced them with modern, fire-proof steel and copper roofing.

* * *

THE FLAG WAS STILL THERE

A short circuit in a spotlight at the base of the dome, August 30, 1948, ignited construction materials on the Capitol's roof. Flames could be seen from the Mall and Pennsylvania Ave. NW, and smoke filled the light shining on the dome. The fire was located very near the flagpole at the center of the West Front. The flag was flying at half staff, mourning the death of Chief Justice Charles Evans Hughes.

An assistant Supreme Court librarian spotted the flames and ran to save the flag from the fire. Before he could reach the flagpole, the man tripped over some rope and twisted his ankle. Despite the failed rescue attempt, the flag was not damaged.

* * *

Cold Secretaries Smoke Up the Place

On a cold February morning in 1932, smoke filled the Capitol office of Rep. Daniel E. Garrett of Texas. An alarm was sounded and several companies of Washington, D.C., firefighters responded.

When fire crews arrived, they found a great deal of smoke, a malfunctioning fireplace, and three cold and very embarrassed office assistants.

Garrett had not come to work that day because he was ill. His secretaries, feeling a winter chill in the air, decided to cozy up the room by building a fire in the fireplace in Garrett's office.

According to the Architect's office, the fireplace likely had not been used for at least 20 years, and the secretaries were unaware that they needed to turn on an electric ventilation fan to create the proper draft. So, when they lit the fire, instead of rising up the chimney, the smoke spread into the office and out into the hallway.

* * *

NO SHORT CUTS

Fire alarms affected Congress even when the fire was somewhere other than the Capitol.

In the days before security barriers restricted access to the roadways on the Capitol grounds, D.C. fire crews routinely used them to save time en route to fires in the neighborhood or other parts of the city.

In 1953, Congress grew tired of the disruptive fire sirens speeding past the Capitol, and told the D.C. Fire Dept. to stop this practice and take the long way around the Capitol grounds.

* * *

FIRE IN THE CAPITOL

A 1930 fire at the Capitol heavily damaged the House document room.

10
TERRORISTS ATTACK

The 20th century brought a new danger to the Capitol. Terrorist attack has become a serious threat for the building, its occupants and the people responsible for their safety. In 1976, Capitol Police began to use metal detectors to screen visitors to the House Gallery. Since then, similar devices have been installed at all public entrances to the Capitol and House and Senate office buildings. Bags and parcels coming into the complex must be x-rayed or hand inspected, and barricades and checkpoints now restrict vehicular access to the Capitol grounds. Security cameras and bomb-sniffing dogs are also in use to prevent terrorist attacks at the Capitol.

Even with increased security and new technology, violence still finds its way into our government's most sacred spaces.

Free Puerto Rico!

On March 1, 1954, five Members of the House were shot and wounded by gunfire from a band of protesters calling for independence for Puerto Rico.

At about 2:30 that afternoon, the armed band of three men and one woman burst into the visitors gallery at the southwest corner of the House Chamber, waving a Puerto Rican flag and shouting "Free Puerto Rico!"

The four opened fire on the Representatives on the floor below, hitting five who were seated in the front row. Wounded in the shooting were Reps. Alvin Bentley of Michigan (struck in the chest and liver), Clifford Davis of Tennessee (leg), Ben F. Jensen of Iowa (shoulder), Kenneth A. Roberts (leg), George Fallon of Maryland (hip).

All four of the shooters were sentenced to 50 years in prison for the attack.

Fights among Members themselves notwithstanding, the 1954 shooting remains the only attack on the Capitol in which Members of Congress were injured.

Bombs for Peace

The Capitol has been the successful target of terrorist bombs three times in its 200-plus-year history. All detonated at night and no one was injured in any of the blasts.

Ironically, all three bombs were set off in the name of peace.

And, by odd coincidence, all three were placed on the Senate side of the Capitol.

The first such explosion took place on July 2, 1915, as World War I raged in Europe.

The bomb, placed through an open window in the Senate Reception Room, heavily damaged the historic room and the adjacent Vice President's Ceremonial Office. The explosion went off just before midnight, when the Capitol was empty, so no one was injured. One guard had checked the room just 10 minutes before the explosion, but was a safe distance away when the bomb went off.

The next day, police in Glen Cove, N.Y., arrested Frank Holt, 40, an instructor of German at Cornell University. Holt confessed to the bombing and a subsequent attack on wealthy financier J.P. Morgan.

Holt told police he set the bomb at the Capitol to protest U.S. sales of arms to combatant countries. The United States was officially neutral at the time, but was selling munitions to the French and British. Holt said he wanted to "shock the country" about "its hidden role" in the war.

The day after the bombing, Holt broke into Morgan's home on Long Island. Morgan was an American financial agent for the Allied countries and helped raise funds for the purchase of weapons and supplies. Holt held Morgan at gunpoint and demanded he use his vast personal and economic resources to stop the American arms sales. When Morgan refused, Holt shot him.

Police were called and Holt was arrested on the spot. He was tried, convicted and sentenced to life in prison in 1916.

(opposite page)

ON WATCH

Capitol Police officers keep watch from above the east portico of the House wing as a news conference takes place on the lawn below.

PHOTO CREDIT:
Jim Berard

The United States officially entered the war in 1917.

Holt died in prison in 1940. Morgan was not seriously wounded by the shooting and outlived his attacker by three years.

At 12:59 a.m. on the morning of March 1, 1971, Capitol Police received the following ominous, anonymous phone call:

"Evacuate the building. You may have gotten other calls like this, but this is real. This is in retaliation for the Laos decision. The bomb will go off in 30 minutes," said the male voice on the phone.

Thirty-three minutes later, 15-20 pounds of dynamite exploded in a Senate men's room.

A radical group known as the Weather Underground, opposed to the war in Vietnam, took credit for the bomb, claiming it was set in protest of the expansion of the war into neighboring Laos. In a letter to the Associated Press, the group said "Lies about the war 'winding down' cannot hide the criminal invasion of Laos."

The Washington Star, in an editorial, called the bombing "a mindless and cowardly act" and accurately predicted that "there will be stiff restrictions on touring of the building now—no more leisurely meandering."

"Extremists exact their penalties in divers (sic) ways," the *Star* editorial concluded.

It cost $118,139 to repair the damage.

Several arrests were made in connection with the blast. One of those arrested was a 21-year-old woman named Leslie Bacon, a known anti-war activist with a group called the Mayday Movement.

The government, however, could not make its case stick, and the charges were dropped. Bacon and five of her colleagues later pled guilty to conspiracy charges in connection with a 1970 attempt to fire-bomb a National City Bank branch in New York.

The 1971 bomb went off in the oldest part of the Capitol, but did little structural damage. The bomb assuaged fears that the building's west center wall, the only section of the original sandstone wall still exposed, was so fragile that it was ready to crumble and send the dome rolling down Capitol Hill. Engineers had even placed timbers on the West Front to brace the old wall.

Architect of the Capitol George M. White said after the blast that the wall proved to be "stronger than you'd think." Nonetheless the wall was fortified in the 1980's.

Anti-war protesters again attacked the Capitol in 1983, this time in response to the U.S. invasion of the Caribbean island of Grenada.

The bomb exploded at 10:58 p.m. in a hallway area outside the Senate Chamber. Hours before, Majority Leader Howard Baker decided to cancel a planned late session of the Senate, so the area was deserted at the time of the blast.

The attackers managed to plant their explosives in a restricted area of the Capitol despite increased security and the installation of metal detectors and x-ray devices in the complex several months earlier.

A group called the Armed Resistance Movement took credit for the bomb. In a communique to National Public Radio, the group said it "purposely aimed our attack at the institutions of imperialist rule rather than individual members of the ruling class and government."

Five years later, seven people were charged with planting the bomb at the Capitol and three related bombings in the Washington area—at the Washington Navy Yard, Ft. Leslie McNair and the U.S. Naval Academy in Annapolis—and four more bombings in New York City. One of those charged was a fugitive who was never brought to trial. The rest became known as the "District 6." In 1990, three of the conspirators pled guilty and were sentenced to jail. Charges were dropped against the other three.

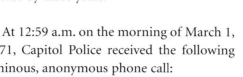

KIDNAP VICTIM

After setting a bomb in the Capitol, a man protesting American support of the Allies in World War I also invaded the home of financier J.P. Morgan, Jr., (pictured)

On a late July day in 2001, Capitol Police were called to the office of freshman Sen. Hillary Rodham Clinton of New York. A man had left a suspicious-looking duffel bag in the Senator's office in the Russell building.

The bag only contained fireworks, police said. Still, they arrested the Pennsylvania man who left the bag and charged him with possession of an incendiary device in the Capitol.

Officers Down

The most deadly attack in the Capitol's history took place on July 24, 1998.

Capitol Police officer Jacob Chestnut was working his station at the ground floor entrance on the House side of the center steps, an entry known as the Document Room Door. As he helped a visitor who had asked for directions, a man tripped the alarm on the metal detector portal. Before the officer could turn around, the man pulled out a pistol and shot Chestnut in the back of the head, taking his life.

Tourists and staffers screamed and ducked for cover. The shooter ran down a side hallway and through a door leading to the office of Republican Whip Tom DeLay. Inside the office he encountered Detective John Gibson, assigned to DeLay's security detail. In an exchange of gunfire, Gibson was struck in the chest and fell, mortally wounded, but continued to fire at the gunman.

Capitol Police arrested Russell E. Weston at the scene. Weston sustained serious wounds in the shootout, and received medical attention from Sen. Bill Frist of Tennessee, a licensed physician.

A tourist was also wounded in the shooting, but not seriously.

The flag-draped caskets of the two slain officers were placed on view in the Capitol Rotunda. Law enforcement officials, government workers and just ordinary Americans stood in line for hours to pay tribute. Memorial flowers filled the center steps on the Capitol's East Front.

The two officers, both veterans of the U.S. Armed Services, were buried with full military honors at Arlington National Cemetery.

Weston was taken to St. Elizabeth's hospital, a mental institution. He was diagnosed with para-

REMEMBERING HEROES

A bronze plaque dedicates a ground-floor Capitol entrance to the memories of Capitol Police officers Jacob Chestnut and John Gibson. The two died in a shootout with a gunman in the adjoining corridors in 1998.

PHOTO CREDIT:
Jeff Lesnik

117

noid schizophrenia and deemed mentally unfit to stand trial.

In tribute to the fallen officers, the Document Room Door was renamed in their honor.

Chestnut and Gibson were the first members of the Capitol Police force to die in action since the force was established in 1828. Another officer, Sgt. Christopher Eney was killed in a training accident in 1984.

★ ★ ★

CONGRESS UNDER GLASS?

Over the years, as security concerns at the Capitol have grown, a number of proposals have been put forward for ensuring the safety of Members of Congress from attacks such as those in 1954 and 1998. A solution often mentioned is enclosing the visitors galleries in the House and Senate with bullet-proof glass. Rep. Joe Waggoner of Texas made just such a recommendation in 1976. Other suggestions included erecting a tall fence to restrict access to the Capitol Grounds.

So far, Congress has resisted these extreme measures. Members are concerned for their own safety but they are also concerned that tough security measures will place too many obstacles between them and the people they serve. Enclosing the galleries or walling off the Capitol would only further distance them from the citizenry.

"We have to accept a certain amount of personal risk as part of the job," Rep. Jolene Unsoeld of Washington said in response to one such suggestion in 1993.

★ ★ ★

9/11

On September 11, 2001, terrorists hijacked four commercial airliners and used them to attack American targets. Two of the jets struck the twin towers of the World Trade Center in New York, causing both towers to collapse and killing some 3,000 innocent people. Nearly 200 more died when another plane was deliberately crashed into the Pentagon, home of the U.S. Department of Defense, in Arlington, Virginia, some 20 minutes later. A fourth jet crashed in rural Pennsylvania after passengers using cell phones caught word of what had happened and attempted to overpower the hijackers. Officials believed that the fourth jet was headed for a target in Washington, most likely the Capitol.

As the morning's events unfolded, Congressional leaders took the unprecedented step of evacuating the Capitol and all House and Senate office buildings. House and Senate leaders were spirited off to a safe, secret location, while other Members of Congress gathered at the Capitol Police headquarters. Later that day, some 100 defiant Representatives and Senators gathered on the center steps of the East Front of the Capitol to announce that the business of government would resume the next day. In a touching demonstration of unity and resolve, the assembled lawmakers spontaneously broke into a chorus of "God Bless America."

Two days later, on September 13, the Capitol was evacuated again when a suspicious package was found in the Senate wing. The package turned out to be harmless, but Members and staff milled about the East Lawn until police gave the all-clear.

After the attacks, additional traffic barriers in the form of concrete planters, pipe sections and Jersey walls were placed on the Capitol grounds to protect against car and truck bombs. Several streets in the area were closed to unauthorized traffic and most trucks were rerouted away from the Capitol.

When President Bush addressed a joint session of Congress shortly after the attacks, a traffic cordon was erected for several blocks around the Capitol. Buses were used as mobile traffic barriers to block off streets.

Military Police units of the National Guard were activated to help Capitol Police screen vehicles entering the Capitol complex, and the terraces along the West Front of the Capitol were closed to tourists. Tours of the Capitol were suspended, and only resumed on a limited basis several months later.

Anthrax!

A month after the September 11th attacks, another threat emerged. On October 15, 2002, a letter to Senate Majority Leader Thomas Daschle contained a suspicious powder that turned out to be tainted with anthrax spores. In a subsequent check of Senate staff, 29 people tested positive for exposure to the disease, but the exposure was confined to workers in Sen. Daschle's office, the adjacent office of Sen. Russ Feingold of Wisconsin and to security personnel who responded when the letter was discovered.

The Daschle letter prompted a complete shutdown of House and Senate offices for several days. Sweeps turned up anthrax spores in mail handling equipment in the Dirksen Senate Office Building and the Longworth and Ford House Office Buildings. Three Members' offices in the Longworth building were contaminated and had to be closed for several weeks.

The worst contamination was confined to the Hart Senate Office Building, where the first letter was delivered to Daschle's office. The building was closed for three months and totally fumigated twice to kill any traces of the dread disease.

The letter to Daschle and another tainted letter addressed to Sen. Patrick Leahy of Vermont, were postmarked in Trenton, New Jersey and listed a fictitious return address. The letters also contam-

inated a Washington, D.C., postal processing facility and two mail handlers later died from exposure to the disease. The facility was closed down for more than a year and all mail addressed to Congress was shipped to Ohio to be decontaminated.

Police had few leads, but were not certain the anthrax-tainted letters originated with the same terrorists who planned and executed the September 11 attacks.

The U.S. Capitol Police: To Serve and Protect

The U.S. Capitol Police force can trace its origins back to 1801, when the first night watchman was hired for the Capitol. The watchman's principal responsibilities were to prevent the theft of building materials and keep livestock from wandering onto the Capitol grounds. If real trouble occurred, he had to call in the Marines. In 1828, a captain and three men were hired as the first Capitol police force to protect the Capitol and Members of Congress. For many years, appointment to the force was done through political channels. Despite efforts of reformers to end the patronage system and professionalize the force, jobs continued to go to those with political connections until the late 20th Century.

College students looking for part-time work made up a large part of the force during this time. They were heavily used as night watchmen in the Capitol. Long-serving Sen. Harry Reid of Nevada worked as a Capitol Police officer during his law school years at George Washington University.

As incidents of violence and terrorism increased the need for tighter security at the Capitol, the patronage police force came under sharper criticism. A number of scandals involving Capitol Police officers did not improve the situation. Students were often caught studying instead of attending to their rounds, and had to be barred from bringing their books to the job. Other officers were found deserting their posts in order to gather three or four at a time in parked cars for cigarette breaks. Local guides accused officers of taking bribes to steer business to certain tour operators.

After the Puerto Rican nationalists shot up the House Chamber in 1954, Congress began supplementing the Capitol force with police from the Metropolitan (Washington, D.C.) Police Department, taking those officers away from duties elsewhere in the city.

A House Appropriations subcommittee in 1959 said the officers of the force were too plentiful in some spots around the Capitol, too scarce in others, woefully untrained, lacking adequate supervision, and even incapable of producing a new training manual.

The force was even criticized for the way its officers dressed. In 1963, several Senators complained that the Capitol Police wore the worst dress uniforms in the country. One Senator said he couldn't tell the guards from the tourists.

(The uniforms didn't bother another Senator, freshman Robert C. Byrd of West Virginia, who said he had no problem recognizing the police officers. His biggest problem, he said, was getting the officers to recognize him.)

The reformers prevailed. The U.S. Capitol Police, now more than 1,250 officers strong, is a well-trained, professional police force, equipped with the latest technology to protect the Capitol, its occupants and visitors. It is also charged with the protection of Members of Congress, their families, and House and Senate officers away from the Capitol as warranted.

In an ironic turnabout from the days after the Puerto Rican attack, the Capitol Police are now giving aid to the Metropolitan Police Department. In 1990, the patrol area of the Capitol force was expanded from the Capitol complex itself to a large part of the surrounding Capitol Hill neighborhood, in order to help stem what was then a growing crime rate in the area. Capitol Police now have arrest authority anywhere in the District of Columbia for crimes committed on Capitol grounds or in one of the Congressional office-buildings, and can make arrests anywhere in the country if they personally witness the crime.

And, in 1988, the U.S. Capitol Police force was voted the best-dressed government security force in the country by the National Association of Uniform Manufacturers and Distributors.

Preparing for the Worst

In order to be prepared for the possible attacks on the Capitol complex, Capitol Police stepped up safety and security measures. Regular evacuation drills are scheduled for each building. The number of visitors to the Capitol has been limited in case an emergency evacuation is needed. In the summer of 2002, escape masks were distributed to Members and staff to be used in case of an attack using chemical or biological weapons by terrorists against the Capitol and Congress. Masks are also to be available in sufficient numbers to protect visitors to the Capitol complex in the event of such an attack.

SECURITY MEASURES

Concrete planters such as these
on the steps of the Russell Senate
Office Building are used throughout the Capitol grounds to protect
against terrorist attacks by car
or truck.

PHOTO CREDIT:
Jim Berard

11
STATUARY STORIES

More than 100 men and women who have made significant contributions to the founding and growth of the American nation are honored with statues in the U.S. Capitol. Most of the statues are gifts from the various states as part of the National Statuary Hall collection. Others are part of the general collection of artwork in the Capitol.

The majority of the statues, like most of the artwork adorning the Capitol, were created and put in place in the 19th Century, and reflect the tastes, ethics, attitudes and politics of that time. White men held all the economic, political and legal power. Slavery was legal in this country for nearly two-thirds of the century, and people of color did not achieve full civil rights until more than half-way through the next century. Women did not hold the right to vote, and, in many places, could not own property. Native Americans were seen either as innocents to be educated and converted, or savages to be tamed or conquered.

It is not surprising, then, that white males dominate the collection, but this fact cannot diminish the contributions made to the country by Washington, Jefferson, Lincoln and the other honorees. And, as the collection grows, we can expect more women and minorities to be so honored.

This chapter is dedicated to some of the more interesting and significant works.

★ ★ ★

THE EYE OF THE BEHOLDER

Mark Twain was impressed by the statues he saw during his first visit to the Capitol in 1854. In a letter to his brother, Orion Clemens, Twain wrote, "The statuary with which [the Capitol] is adorned is most beautiful."

On the other hand, British sculptor Sir Jacob Epstein visited the Capitol a century later and declared the building had more bad statues than he had ever seen before in one place.

★ ★ ★

Samuel Adams (1722-1803)—"The Father of the American Revolution," Sam Adams was a leader in the independence movement in Massachusetts. As a young student at Harvard, Adams was exposed to the works of philosophers such as John Locke, who stressed the inalienable rights of individuals over the divine right of kings. Adams' fiery rhetoric heated the passions of his fellow Bostonians and led to such protests as the Boston Tea Party.

Adams' statue, in marble by Ann Whitney, was donated in 1876.

William Jennings Bryan (1860-1925)—A leader in the populist cause, William Jennings Bryan of Nebraska was known as the "Great Commoner." After serving two terms in the House of Representatives, Bryan lost a bid for the Senate, but used his position as a newspaperman to rise to prominence in national politics. An unsuccessful candidate for President in 1896, Bryan continued to be a force in the Democratic Party, eventually landing the office of Secretary of State in the Cabinet of President Woodrow Wilson.

Bryan may be best known for his "Cross of Gold" speech calling for the increased circulation of silver coins to help the depressed farm economy, and his prosecution of Tennessee schoolteacher John Scopes for teaching the theory of evolution. The Scopes trial is the basis for the renowned stage play *Inherit the Wind*.

The bronze statue of William Jennings Bryan, by sculptor Rudulph Evans, was donated to the national collection by Nebraska in 1937.

★ ★ ★

KEEPING THEM CLEAN

The statues in the Capitol present a challenge to the engineers and custodians charged with their care.

The simple act of dusting the statues can be complicated. When ordinary feather dusters scratched the figures, the dusters were changed to ostrich plumes.

Vandals provide additional challenges. Marks made with oily substances such as lipstick and crayon are easily absorbed into the porous marble. Conservators use a poultice of corn meal to draw out the stains.

Some statues are bigger targets than others. Vandals used to regularly break off the trigger guard on the rifle held by the figure of Stephen A. Austin.

Vandalism is not a new phenomenon in the Capitol. An item in the Washington Star *of January 26, 1897, told of a man caught striking a match on the statue of Daniel Webster. The vandal was arrested, taken to a nearby precinct house and fined five dollars.*

The article reports the event was the second match attack on Webster that week.

★ ★ ★

Charles Carroll of Carrollton (1737-1832)— When he signed his name to the Declaration of Independence, Charles Carroll of Carrollton joined the rest of the Continental Congress in staking his life, fortune and sacred honor. In doing so, he placed more at risk than any of the other signers. Carroll was considered the wealthiest man in the colonies at the time. (He used "of Carrollton" to distinguish himself from other Charles Carrolls, including his father.) After the Revolutionary War, Carroll served three years in the Senate (1789-1792).

At his death in 1832, at age 95, Carroll was the last surviving signer of the Declaration of Independence.

His bronze statue by Richard E. Brooks was donated in 1903 by the State of Maryland.

Fr. Damien of Hawaii (born Joseph de Veuster, 1840-1889)—A Catholic missionary from Belgium, Father Damien worked with the inhabitants of the Hawaiian island of Molokai. Many in Fr. Damien's flock suffered from Hansen's disease,

more commonly known as leprosy. After 11 years on Molokai, Fr. Damien himself contracted the disease. His statue, donated by the State of Hawaii in 1969, was done by Marisol (born Marisol Escobar). The bronze work shows the priest in his later years and displays some of the effects of the disease on Fr. Damien's body.

Most striking about the statue is the boxy shape of the subject's torso. Sculptor Marisol is known for works that retain much of the shape of the original block. (Although this statue is in bronze, most of Marisol's works are carved from blocks of wood.) The sculpture's shape is the source of an often-repeated myth about the statue and Fr. Damien's life. According to the myth, Fr. Damien wore a wooden frame under his robes to keep his clothing from irritating the sores on his skin. There is no evidence to support this.

"Not a word of truth to it," said Curator Barbara Wolanin. The story sprung up as an explanation of the statue's odd shape by a Capitol security officer not familiar with Marisol's style.

Fr. Damien's statue in the Capitol is one of two identical works. The other is displayed in front of the State Capitol in Honolulu.

Jefferson Davis (1808-1889) and **Robert E. Lee** (1807-1870)—Standing across from each other in Statuary Hall are tributes to two leaders of the Confederacy, Jefferson Davis and Robert E. Lee. Davis served as Senator from Mississippi and Secretary of War before leaving Washington to accept the Presidency of the Confederate States of America. Lee, a West Point graduate and the former Superintendent of the military academy, commanded the Confederate army during the Civil War. What is significant about these statues is that they honor two men who led the secession movement against the United States government. The fact that both of these men have been given places of honor in the U.S. Capitol is a tribute to the nation's ability to heal its divisions and work together for a better future.

THE MISSIONARY OF MOLOKAI

Fr. Damien DeVeuster, a Belgian priest who ministered to the people of the Hawaiian Islands of Molokai, is honored with one of Hawaii's two statues in the National Statuary Hall Collection.

PHOTO CREDIT:
Jeff Lesnik

Davis' bronze statue is by Augustus Lukeman. It was donated to the national collection by Mississippi in 1931. Lee's statue, also in bronze, was given by Lee's home state of Virginia in 1934. It is by sculptor Edward V. Valentine.

Robert Fulton (1765-1815)—Another inventor honored in the Capitol is Robert Fulton. An artist early in his life, Fulton moved to Europe and became fascinated with machines and steam engines. One of Fulton's inventions was a "diving boat" or submarine he named the *Nautilus,* but he could not interest any government to buy his invention.

He is best known for his development of a steam-powered riverboat. Dubbed the *Clermont* after the family estate of his friend and sponsor, Robert Livingston, Fulton is generally considered the inventor of the steamboat.

Fulton's bronze statue by Howard Roberts stands in Statuary Hall, but Fulton's invention was so important to 19th Century America that he is honored in two other places in the Capitol. Fulton's image can be found in the *Apotheosis of Washington* fresco on the ceiling of the Rotunda, and in another Brumidi work honoring inventors in the corridor just outside room S-211 (formerly occupied by the Committee on Patents).

Fulton's patron for the *Clermont*, Livingston, also has a statue in the Capitol.

* * *

GOUVERNEUR WASHINGTON?

In the Capitol Rotunda, near the portal leading to Statuary Hall, stands a copy of a statue reputed to be the closest likeness of George Washington in existence. The original stands in the Virginia state capitol in Richmond. The statue was created by the renowned French sculptor Jean-Antoine Houdon, under commission from the Virginia General Assembly.

Houdon spent two weeks at Washington's home at Mount Vernon in 1785, making plaster casts and detailed measurements of Washington's face and body. (Martha Washington's six-year-old granddaughter, Nellie Custis, walked in on Houdon as he was applying plaster to Washington, who was covered in a sheet. The girl became distraught because she thought the General had died.)

The finished work depicts Washington in his Continental Army uniform, a sword in one hand and a cane in the other, to represent the balance between military power and civil authority. Fasces—an ancient symbol of democracy from Roman times—and a plow stand at his side, to represent Washington's service in the government and his private life as a Virginia planter.

Sherwin McRae, author of the official history of the statue by commission of the Virginia legislature, wrote that many distinguished persons who knew Washington personally judged Houdon's work a most accurate likeness. These included Thomas Jefferson, Benjamin Franklin, and the Marquis de Lafayette. A number of observers, though, have noticed something peculiar about the appearance of Washington's legs.

According to some accounts, the body of the statue is not Washington's at all, but that of Gouverneur Morris of Pennsylvania, one of the framers of the Constitution. While serving as an American diplomat in Paris, Morris was recruited to pose for Houdon wearing Washington's uniform and boots. Morris was of slightly smaller stature than Washington, and had an artificial right leg, which required him to wear a built-up shoe. When Morris put on Washington's boots, his right leg was slightly shorter than the left. That difference, some observers say, is reflected in the statue.

Defenders of Houdon's work dispute this view. Nowhere is this defense more passionate than in Richmond, where Houdon's original stands. The Capitol Hostesses, who provide tours and assist visitors to Virginia's capitol building, concede that Morris did pose for Houdon in Washington's uniform, but they con-

THE LENGTH OF A LEG

A copy of Jean-Antoine Houdon's statue of George Washington stands in the Rotunda. The work is considered by many to be the best likeness of Washington ever created, but some observers contend the sculptor made Washington's right leg longer than his left.

PHOTO CREDIT:
Jeff Lesnik

tend that the sculptor based the statue's dimensions on the precise measurements he made of Washington's body during his visit to Mount Vernon. The body is all Washington's, they insist. So, it is up to the eye of the beholder to determine if the statue is a true depiction of George Washington, or the head of a President on the body of a Gouverneur.

John Gorrie (1802-1855)—A physician, John Gorrie worked along the Gulf Coast of Florida, battling mosquito-borne diseases and the stifling heat and humidity that slowed his patients' recovery. Gorrie urged the draining of swamps and the use of mosquito netting to slow the spread of disease. He also pioneered the use of refrigeration to cool hospital rooms.

At first Gorrie used fans blowing over blocks of ice to cool patients, but ice had to be brought in from colder climates many miles away from the coast. So, Gorrie set out to develop a way to freeze water artificially. In 1845, Gorrie gave up his medical practice to devote all of his time to his invention. In 1851 he was granted a patent for his ice-making machine.

The marble statue of Gorrie is by sculptor C.A. Pillars.

John Hanson (1715-1783)—John Hanson of Maryland could be considered America's real first President. In 1781 and 1782, Hanson presided over Congress under the Articles of Confederation and held the title "President of the United States in Congress Assembled." As the young nation's first chief executive, Hanson helped establish a postal system, a uniform system of coinage and the first national bank. He also organized the first cabinet, issued the first Presidential military orders, and issued the first Thanksgiving Day proclamation.

Hanson died in 1783, six years before George Washington took office as the first President of the United States under the new Constitution. Hanson's statue, in bronze, is by Richard Brooks, and was given to the Capitol in 1903.

Mother Joseph (1823-1902)—In 1843, French Canadian Esther Pariseau was sent by her father to join the religious order, the Sisters of Charity of Providence, in Montreal. In 1856, she led a group of five sisters to the Pacific Northwest, where they established hospitals, schools and orphanages. The sisters raised money for these projects by touring the lumber camps of the region asking for donations.

Mother Joseph was an able carpenter and architect, and often took a direct involvement in the design and construction of the buildings that would house the institutions she founded.

In 1953, 41 years after her death, the American Institute of Architects declared Mother Joseph "The First Architect of the Pacific Northwest."

The bronze statue of Mother Joseph in the Capitol is by Felix W. de Weldon.

King Kamehameha I (c. 1758-1819)—Hawaii's greatest king, Kamehameha I, united all the Hawaiian Islands under his rule and opened the islands to contact with the rest of the world through trade. His bronze statue is by Thomas R. Gould. A duplicate stands in front of the Iolani Palace in Honolulu, former seat of the Royal Hawaiian government.

The Rev. Dr. Martin Luther King, Jr. (1929-1968)—The first African American individually represented in the Capitol's art collection is the humanitarian, minister and social activist, the Rev. Dr. Martin Luther King, Jr.

Standing in a place of honor in the Rotunda, the bronze bust is by artist John Wilson.

King was a charismatic leader of the African American struggle for equal rights in the 1960's. King disavowed violence as a means of social change, choosing instead to use peaceful means, including marches, strikes, boycotts, sit-ins and public rallies to attract attention and support for the cause.

A winner of the Nobel Peace Prize in 1964, King was assassinated during a visit to Memphis, Tennessee, in 1968.

The King sculpture was installed in 1986, the same year King's birthday was first observed as a national holiday.

Since the addition of the King bust to the Capitol, efforts have intensified to add more artwork honoring important African Americans. In 2002, the Senate added a portrait of Sen. Blanche Bruce of Mississippi, the first African American to serve a full term in the U.S. Senate, to its collection. A year later, the House approved the commission of a portrait of its first African-American Member, Rep. Joseph Hayne Rainey of South Carolina.

Abraham Lincoln (1809-1865)—The Great Emancipator, the Savior of the Union, and the 16th President of the United States, Abraham Lincoln is represented in several works around the Capitol.

A 40-inch representation of Lincoln's head in marble stands in the Crypt. The work was done by Gutzon Borglum in 1908. Borglum went on to design and supervise the carving of the heads of four Presidents on Mt. Rushmore, near Rapid City, South Dakota. Four other Borglum works are also displayed in the Capitol.

A bust of Lincoln, with shoulders draped in a Roman toga, stands on the third floor of the Senate wing. The work, in marble, was done by Sarah Fisher Ames in 1868.

The most remarkable sculpture of Lincoln, though, is a life-size, full-length marble statue in the Rotunda. Sculptor Vinnie Ream was only a teenager when she persuaded the President to allow her to sculpt a clay model of his head. Lincoln took pity on the young woman because she was from a poor family and allowed her to spend a half-hour a day at the White House for five months as she worked on her model. Ream's work was almost finished when, on April 14, 1865, Lincoln was fatally shot while attending a play at Ford's Theater.

A year later, Congress wanted to commission a statue to pay tribute to the slain President. It chose Ream, then only 20, to do the work and awarded her the $10,000 commission. It marked the first time the federal government ever awarded such a commission to a woman.

Ream's statue shows Lincoln standing, eyes gazing downward. He holds a copy of the Emancipation Proclamation in his right hand. Ream's work captures both the greatness and the melancholy of the martyred President.

The Lincoln statue is one of three sculptures by Ream on display in the Capitol.

NATIVE TRIBUTES

Native Americans are represented by three statues in the National Statuary Hall collection, three marble busts in the Senate wing, and one bronze bust in the House wing:

Sequoyah (1770-1843)—Sequoyah developed an alphabet for his native Cherokee people, allowing them to write and read in their own language. He served as a liaison between his tribe and the government in Washington and worked to improve living conditions for Cherokees displaced from their lands in the east. Two species of redwood trees were named for him. Sequoyah's statue was donated by Oklahoma in 1917. It was done in bronze by sculptors Vinnie Ream and G. Julian Zolnay.

Washakie (c. 1800-1900)—The statue of Washakie is one of the newest and most striking additions to the statuary collection, donated by the state of Wyoming in 2001. Respected for his prowess in battle and his efforts to secure land and education for his Shoshone people, Washakie spoke several Native American and European languages. The Washakie statue is done in bronze by Dave McGary.

**TO THE
STARS AND BACK**

Astronaut Jack Swigert was a member of the crew of the 1970 Apollo 13 moon mission whose dramatic rescue had the nation holding its breath. Elected to the House in 1982, Swigert died before he could take his seat in Congress.

PHOTO CREDIT:
Jeff Lesnik

Buffalo and Flat Mouth (Dates unknown)— Pee-Che-Kir (Buffalo) and Aysh-Ke-Bah-Ke-Ko-Zhay (Flat Mouth) were Chippewa leaders who came to Washington in 1855, heading a delegation of 14 representatives of Minnesota and Wisconsin tribes to negotiate a treaty with President Franklin Pierce. During their month's stay in Washington, the two Native American leaders sat for Italian sculptor Francis Vincenti, who created marble busts of them. The two busts now stand in a third floor lobby of the Senate wing, near the entrance to the Press Gallery. A bronze copy of the Pee-Che-Kir bust is displayed on the third floor of the House wing.

Charles Curtis (1860-1936)—A Republican from Kansas, Curtis was of Kaw-Osage ancestry. Elected to the House in 1893, Curtis served in that body for 14 years, then moved to the Senate for three non-consecutive terms. In 1928, Curtis was elected Vice President of the United States on the ticket with Herbert Hoover. His marble bust is displayed in the Senate wing as part of the Vice Presidential Bust Collection.

Will Rogers (1879-1935)—Humorist, political commentator and homespun philosopher, Will Rogers entertained America during the years of the Great Depression. Dubbed "The Cherokee Kid" and proud of his Native American heritage, Rogers lifted Americans' spirits—in personal appearances, radio programs and motion pictures—with his pointed but lighthearted comments on current affairs. Congress was a particularly favorite target. He often referred to Members of Congress as "professional joke makers."

Rogers' bronze likeness by Jo Davidson, donated in 1939, was placed on the second floor of the Capitol, just outside the door to the House Chamber, so he could continue to keep an eye on Congress.

★ ★ ★

Florence R. Sabin (1871-1953)—In the early 20th Century, the practice of medicine was considered a profession for men, and no place for a woman. Then came Florence Sabin and others like her. A graduate of Smith College, Sabin attended Johns Hopkins Medical School in Baltimore and became the first woman to graduate from that institution. She went on to teach anatomy at the school, and, in 1917, she was awarded a full professorship, the first woman to win such a post at an American school of medicine. She was elected the first woman president of the American Association of Anatomists in 1924 and became the first woman to earn lifetime membership in the National Academy of Sciences.

In 1925, Dr. Sabin was selected to head the Division of Cellular Studies at the Rockefeller Institute for Medical Research in New York. She retired in 1938, but came out of retirement six years later to help revamp the public health laws in her home state of Colorado.

Her bronze statue is by Joy Buba, and was donated to the NSH Collection in 1959.

Roger Sherman (1721-1793)—Of all the men who had a hand in creating our nation's government and its body of laws, only one, Roger Sherman of Connecticut, signed all four of the major documents leading to the establishment of an independent United States of America. A member of the Continental Congress, Sherman signed the Association of 1774, the Declaration of Independence, the Articles of Confederation and the Constitution of the United States.

At the Constitutional Convention in 1787, Sherman came up with the idea that broke the deadlock over the makeup in Congress. He suggested a bicameral—two chamber—system, consisting of the Senate, where all states are represented equally, and the House of Representatives, where representation varies depending on the size of a state's population.

Sherman served in the House during the First Congress of the United States (1789-1791), which created the Bill of Rights. He was elected to the Senate in 1791 and served until his death two years later.

Sherman's statue in bronze is by Chauncey B. Ives.

Jack Swigert (1931-1982)—"Houston we have a problem." By those words most people know the plight of the Apollo 13 moonshot in 1970. The mission and the lives of the three astronauts aboard the spacecraft were jeopardized by an equipment malfunction. One of those three astronauts was John L. "Jack" Swigert.

After many tense hours and extraordinarily heroic efforts by the crew in space and their support team on the ground, the three astronauts were returned safely to earth after nearly six days in space.

After leaving the space program, Swigert came to Capitol Hill, where he joined the staff of the House Committee on Space, Science and Technology. In 1982, Swigert ran for and was elected to a Congressional seat from Colorado, but died before he could take office.

His statue is a gift of the State of Colorado. It was done in bronze by George and Mark Lundeen.

* * *

THE KANSAS SWITCHEROO

Some states that were quick to send their quota of two statues to Statuary Hall later regretted their haste. In some cases, the 19th Century politicians represented by the statues were later eclipsed by other more prominent people from the state. In other cases, states saw the need to recognize the accomplishments of women and people of color in a collection that honors mostly white males. So, states won the right to swap out the original contributions for new statues, if they so wished.

Kansas was the first to take advantage of the opportunity, choosing to replace the statues of Sen. John James Ingalls and Gov. George Washington Glick with those of President Dwight D. Eisenhower and pioneer aviator Amelia Earhart.

* * *

Brigham Young (1801-1877)—The leader of the Mormon migration to the West and founder of the Territory of Deseret, Brigham Young's image is preserved in a marble work by Mahonri Young. Brigham Young organized the movement of some 70,000 Mormons to settlements he established throughout the West. By 1896, the Territory of Deseret became the State of Utah, which donated the statue in 1950.

Suffragettes in a Tub

Along the Rotunda's northwest wall stands an unusual statue of three important women.

Busts of Susan B. Anthony, Elizabeth Cady Stanton, and Lucretia Mott, early leaders in the movement to secure equal rights for women, are carved from a single block of white Italian marble.

The portraits of the three women are completed only down to just below their shoulders, giving them the appearance of standing in chest-deep water. This has led some detractors to dub the work "Three Women in a Tub."

Such barbs aside, the three women made profound contributions in the struggle to win voting rights and equal treatment under the law for women. The sculpture was a gift of the National Women's Party and was presented to Congress in 1921, just one year after women won the right to vote. For 75 years the work was displayed in the Crypt, until Congress voted in 1996 to move it upstairs into the Rotunda. It was moved to its present location the next year.

Artist Adelaide Johnson based the portraits on individual busts she had done of the same women for the 1893 World's Columbian Exhibition in Chicago.

The massive statue weighs 14,000 pounds (6,364 kilograms).

Banished Satues

Times change, tastes change and the Capitol's art collection must change with them. Several statues which graced the Capitol for many years, eventually fell out of favor and were banished to other venues, or to oblivion.

The most famous of these is Horatio Greenough's Olympian sculpture of George Washington, commissioned by Congress in 1832 and installed in the Rotunda in 1841. Based on one of the Seven Wonders of the Ancient World, the statue of the Greek god Zeus at the temple at Olympia, the work depicts Washington seated, stripped to the waist, wearing a toga, sandals, and a crown of laurels. Many Americans of the day could not accept a monument depicting a half-naked, imperial Washington. Critics enjoyed poking fun at the statue. One wit imagined Washington to be saying, "Give me liberty or give me death, but for God's sake give me some clothes!"

The work was later removed to the Capitol grounds. It now resides in the Smithsonian Institution's Museum of American History.

Another Greenough work, *Rescue,* graced the center steps on the Capitol's East Front for over 100 years. Most likely inspired by an illustration in a 1784 text on the life of pioneer Daniel Boone, *Rescue* depicts a white frontiersman wrestling with a hostile native who threatened his family. It was removed to storage in 1958 when work began on the East Front extension and has been away from public view ever since.

Also banished from the Capitol is Luigi Perisco's *Discovery of America.* The work shows Christopher Columbus, standing tall and holding a world globe in his outstretched hand while a young, underdressed Native American woman crouches beneath his arm. One observer said the statue "depicts Columbus as a high school coach dashing into the girls' shower room demanding to know who let the air out of the volleyball."

Discovery was removed from the East Front with *Rescue* in 1958.

Two other Perisco works, *War* and *Peace*, once stood in recesses flanking the center doors on the East Front. Removed in 1958 with the others, the two statues had badly deteriorated, so Congress ordered replacements. The new works were similar to the originals, but not exact copies.

Old *War* and *Peace*, *Rescue* and *Discovery* were all crated up and placed in storage at the Capitol power plant. In 1976 they were turned over to the Smithsonian Institution for storage. During the transfer, workers dropped *Rescue* and heavily damaged it. The four works banished from the East Front are now stored at the Smithsonian's service facility in Maryland.

BANISHED FROM THE CAPITOL

Horatio Greenough's statue of
George Washington *(top)*;
Greenough's *Rescue (bottom left)* ;
and Luigi Perisco's *Discovery of
America (bottom right).*

12
AROUND THE GROUNDS

The Capitol sits on nearly 60 acres of landscaped parkland featuring colorful flowers, manicured lawns and historic trees. In the mid-19th Century, Congress hired Frederick Law Olmsted, who also designed New York's Central Park, to bring order to the chaos that surrounded the Capitol at the time. Olmsted created an idyllic green space around the building. The architect was mindful, though, that the Capitol was the star of the show, and made sure that the grounds complimented the building, and did not hide or distract from it.

The East Plaza

Once a jammed parking lot, the Capitol's East Plaza is still accessible by car, but only Members of Congress and certain staff can park there, and only for short periods. For security as well as aesthetic reasons, traffic on the East Plaza has been restricted since the 1980's. The restriction on parking was intended to give the plaza a more open, pleasing appearance, although the addition of hydraulic gates and concrete security barriers around the plaza made it less welcoming.

The plaza features include two ornate shelters left over from the days when streetcars served the Capitol.

*   *   *

DRY BONES

When workers began to excavate for the extension of the East Front in 1959, they came across a number of bones buried near the Capitol's walls.

They were later identified as pig, turkey and ox bones. Historians speculate they were left over from the celebrations that followed the laying of the original cornerstone in 1793 or the cornerstone for the new House and Senate wings in 1851.

*   *   *

Welcoming Visitors

In June, 2000, ground was broken for the latest addition to the Capitol, the Capitol Visitors Center. Located underground beneath the East Plaza, the visitors center will provide 580,000 square feet of space on three levels for exhibits, amenities, security functions and offices.

The center is being built below ground in order to provide maximum convenient access to the Capitol without obstructing or detracting from the view of the historic building.

The new facility will be able to accommodate as many as 5,000 visitors at a time and allow about 1,500 visitors an hour to tour the Capitol and another 700 an hour to visit the House and Senate galleries. (Some three million visitors came to see the Capitol in 2000. At peak times, the building could experience as many as 18,000 visitors a day.)

A Swamp, a Triangle and an Elm Tree

Television news crews love shots with the Capitol dome in the background, and Members of Congress are always happy to accommodate them. As a result, three areas on the Capitol grounds, with clear shots of the building and its famous dome, are designated sites for TV interviews, news conferences and other media events. They are known as the House Triangle, the Senate Swamp and the Elm Tree site.

The Senate Swamp is located on a tree-covered area of the East Lawn opposite the Senate steps. The area is equipped with electrical power and direct line hook-ups for most of the TV networks to allow live coverage from the site. (Reporters dubbed it the Swamp because the grassy area could become very muddy when heavily used during wet weather. Paving stones have since been added to the site, making it less swampy, but the name has stuck.)

(opposite page)

HIGH-FLYING TECHNOLOGY

A 1990 hearing before the House Aviation Subcommittee on the applications of tiltrotor technology for commercial air travel included a demonstration by the experimental XV-15 aircraft on the East Plaza of the Capitol. Tiltrotor aircraft combine the flying capabilities of helicopters and fixed-wing airplanes. The military adopted this technology for the V-22 Osprey.

PHOTO CREDIT:
Bell Helicopter/Textron

The Elm Tree site is similarly located on the lawn opposite the House steps and has the same facilities as the Senate Swamp. It is named for the large elm tree that shades it.

The House Triangle is a triangular (!) patch of grass near the Elm Tree site. It has an unobstructed view of the Capitol and its dome, and therefore is a very popular location for outdoor news conferences. Electrical power and transmission lines can be run from the hookups at the nearby Elm Tree site.

Historic Trees

Over the years, 85 memorial trees have been planted on the East Lawn to commemorate distinguished individuals and events. Trees have been planted to honor George Washington, the Boy Scouts, and every First Lady since Lady Bird Johnson. Five crabapple trees honor the memory of the five Sullivan brothers of Waterloo, Iowa, who enlisted in the Navy and died together in World War II.

A handful of the commemorative trees were among the 76 trees removed to make way for the new visitors center. All of them were examined and were found to be diseased or near the end of their life cycles. Workers were able to relocate eight of the memorial trees to other parts of the lawn.

When the visitors center project is completed, additional trees will be planted on the East Lawn, and the grounds will have more trees than it had when the project began.

The West Lawn

Spreading out like a green carpet beneath the West Front of the Capitol, is the West Lawn.

Originally fenced off by Charles Bulfinch then expanded by Olmsted, the lawn now provides an inviting link between the Capitol grounds and the National Mall to the west.

Every four years the West Front is the site of the Presidential Inauguration, and the West Lawn is covered with spectators. The lawn is intermittently used for other events and public rallies. In the summer, the National Symphony Orchestra performs free concerts for Memorial Day, Independence Day and Labor Day. The annual Independence Day concert is televised nationally and culminates with fireworks on the Mall.

The Capitol Christmas Tree

The practice of erecting a Christmas tree on the Capitol lawn dates back as far as 1919. The modern tradition dates to 1964, when a live Douglas Fir was planted on the lawn as the permanent holiday tree.

The tree was decorated each Christmas through 1967. In 1968, the tree died from disease and was removed. Each year a new freshly cut tree is brought to the West Lawn and decorated for the holidays. Each year since 1970, the U.S. Forest

Service has provided a tree from a different National Forest for this purpose.

The annual lighting ceremony is led by the Speaker of the House.

Summer House

Tucked into a shady area off the northwest corner of the Capitol is the Summer House. The small, red brick building houses a drinking fountain and provides a cool shelter from the hot Washington summers.

The building was added to the grounds about 1880 to give travelers and visitors to the Capitol a place to rest and take a cool drink. Water originally came from a natural spring, but now comes from the city's water system.

Grant, Garfield and Peace

Standing at the foot of Capitol Hill and looking west toward the Washington Monument is an equestrian statue of General—later President—Ulysses S. Grant. The bronze statue shows Grant, in his Union Army uniform, mounted on a horse, and flanked on either side by Union soldiers from the Civil War.

Just south of Gen. Grant stands a statue of another President. On a traffic island where Maryland Avenue meets First St. SW, at the west edge of the Capitol lawn, stands the image of James Garfield, Representative, Senator-elect, and 20th President of the United States.

Elected to the White House in 1880, Garfield had held office only four months when he was fatally shot at the Baltimore and Potomac Railroad depot in Washington. Garfield's statue stands in clear view of the scene of his shooting. The National Gallery of Art now occupies the site.

North of the Garfield statue, at the end of Pennsylvania Ave. NW, stands the Peace Monument, erected in memory of the men who lost their lives at sea during the Civil War. The 44-foot tall monument dates to 1878, and bears allegorical figures representing Grief, History, Victory, and Peace, and the Roman gods Mars (war) and Neptune (sea).

In 1959, the location of the Garfield statue and the Peace Monument drew criticism from some Members of Congress who said they were obstructing traffic near the Capitol. Rep. Basil Whitener of South Carolina argued unsuccessfully that the two monuments should be moved to a less-traveled location. Whitener brought the matter up again two years later, but this time targeted only the Garfield statue. (He didn't want to appear to be anti-Peace.) Whitener's efforts fizzled again when Northern colleagues accused him of simply trying to remove a monument to a Yankee President.

THE HERO OF APPOMATTOX

A statue of General U.S. Grant astride his horse stands at the foot of Capitol Hill. New Presidents taking the oath of office on the Capitol's West Front are greeted by the sight of Grant's back—and his horse's tail.

PHOTO CREDIT:
Jeff Lesnik

BARTHOLDI'S FOUNTAIN

Frédéric Auguste Bartholdi, the artist who designed the Statue of Liberty, created this ornate fountain for the American Centennial celebration in Philadelphia in 1876. The government bought the fountain and moved it to the Capitol grounds.

★ ★ ★

VIEW FROM THE TOP

Since 1981, Presidents have been sworn in on the West Front of the Capitol. After taking the oath of office, the President turns and delivers his inaugural address to the crowd assembled on the West Lawn. Facing out toward the National Mall, over the sea of admiring faces on the lawn below and to the monuments to two of our greatest Presidents, Washington and Lincoln, beyond, the nation's Chief Executive, the Head of State, the Commander-in-Chief of the Armed Forces comes face-to-face, so to speak, with the statue of General Grant.

Since the statue is facing away from the Capitol, the President gets a great view of the east end of the General's westbound horse.

It must be a humbling experience.

★ ★ ★

Fountain Service

An historic fountain graces a triangular corner of the Capitol grounds along Independence Avenue west of the Rayburn House Office Building.

Created in 1876 by sculptor Frédéric Auguste Bartholdi, who designed the Statue of Liberty, the fountain was first displayed at the U.S. Centennial Exhibition in Philadelphia. When the exhibition closed, the federal government purchased the work for the Capitol grounds.

The Bartholdi Fountain stands 30 feet tall and weighs nearly 40 tons. It was originally displayed west of the Capitol, at about the center line of the Mall, on what was then part of the grounds of the U.S. Botanic Garden. It was removed in 1927 and five years later re-erected on its current site, now called Bartholdi Park.

Several other fountains grace the grounds around the Capitol complex. At the north end of Senate Park, between the Capitol and Union Station, is a fountain built above an underground garage serving the nearby Senate Office Buildings.

The unimaginatively named Senate Garage Fountain was installed in 1932. The fountain and the reflecting pool below it accent the view of the Capitol from the north. On nights when the fountain is operating, a changing prism of colored lights further adds to its charm and beauty.

Two smaller fountains can be found on the House side of the grounds, south of the Rayburn and Longworth House Office Buildings. Like their Senate cousin, these fountains also are located in park areas above underground garages. Less visible than the Senate fountain, the two House garage fountains flank the approach to the Capitol from the south.

A Garden in the City

Established in 1820, the U.S. Botanic Garden is a museum of living plants. The garden covers nearly two acres of land in the southwest corner of the Capitol grounds. The heart of the facility is the conservatory at Maryland Ave. and First St. SW. The glass-enclosed greenhouse contains nearly 4,000 plants from every corner and every climate of the world.

Taft Memorial Carillon

A 100-foot tower "of simple strength and quiet dignity" stands in Senate Park north of the Capitol. This is the Robert A. Taft Memorial Carillon.

Dedicated in 1959, the tower is a memorial to the late Senator from Ohio, the only such monument to a U.S. Senator on the Capitol Grounds.

The tower, of Tennessee marble, is 100 feet high, 32 feet wide and 11 feet thick. It was designed by architect Douglas W. Orr. At the base is

a 10-foot statue of Taft by sculptor Wheeler Williams.

The tower houses an automated carillon consisting of 27 bells cast in France, the largest weighing seven tons. The carillon plays a patriotic melody at the top of each hour and chimes at 15, 30 and 45 minutes past each hour.

The inscription on the tower reads, "This Memorial to Robert A. Taft, presented by the people to the Congress of the United States, stands as a tribute to the honesty, indomitable courage and high principles of free government symbolized by his life."

The memorial was paid for through private contributions.

(Read more about Taft in Chapter 2.)

THE NATIONAL GREENHOUSE *(left)*

The U.S. Botanic Garden occupies two acres just west of the Capitol. The garden's centerpiece is the conservatory, which houses plants from all over the world.

PHOTO CREDIT:
Jim Berard

A TRIBUTE TO "MR. REPUBLICAN"

A memorial carillon tower on the northern edge of the Capitol grounds stands as a tribute to Sen. Robert A. Taft of Ohio. The memorial was dedicated in 1959.

PHOTO CREDIT:
Jim Berard

13

H.O.B.S. AND S.O.B.S.
THE HOUSE AND SENATE OFFICE BUILDINGS

By the end of the 19th Century, House and Senate quarters in the Capitol were becoming cramped. Some Congressmen even rented office space in nearby buildings. It soon became obvious that Congress would have to either further expand the Capitol or build auxiliary office buildings to provide its Members with desperately needed office space. They chose the latter.

In March, 1901, Congress authorized the Architect of the Capitol to draw up plans for two Congressional office buildings. A New York architectural firm, Carrre and Hastings, was hired to build what were later to become the Cannon House Office Building and the Russell Senate Office Building.

There are now six such office buildings providing space for Representatives, Senators and their staffs. Three of them, serving the Senate, are located north of the Capitol along Constitution Ave. Three others, serving the House, are along Independence Ave. south of the Capitol.

Russell Senate Office Building

The original Senate Office Building, now named the Richard B. Russell Senate Office Building, is nearly a mirror image of its sister structure, the Cannon House Office Building, built across the Capitol's east lawn, although there was a significant difference when they were first built. The House building is a four-sided structure built around a central courtyard. The Senate did not need as many offices as the House, so the Senate building was constructed in a U-shape, with wings along Constitution and Delaware Avenues and C Street NE. The distinction was only tempoary. The Senate building's First Street wing was added 20 years later, making the two buildings nearly identical in shape and size.

The two buildings were fitted with the most modern features of their time, including steam heat, individual lavatories with hot and cold run-

ning water, electric lighting, forced-air ventilation and telephones.

The Russell Building is also home to the Senate Caucus Room, (usually referred to by television reporters as the "*historic* Senate Caucus Room"). Several high-profile Senate hearings have been held in this room, including an inquiry into the sinking of the Titanic in 1912, the Army-McCarthy hearings in 1954, the Watergate hearings in 1973 and the Iran-Contra hearings in 1987.

The Senate Office Building opened in 1909, and was renamed for Sen. Richard Brevard Russell in 1972.

★ ★ ★

ONE S.O.B. TO ANOTHER

For nearly 50 years, the Russell building was the only office building serving the Senate, and was known simply as the Senate Office Building, or by the less-than-flattering initials "S.O.B."

When future President Harry Truman served in the Senate, he told his constituents from Missouri that, if they wanted to write him a letter, they would only have to address it to "Truman, S.O.B., Washington, D.C."

When the Dirksen building opened in 1958, it was called the New Senate Office Building. The Russell building then became known as the "Old S.O.B." until it was rechristened with its current name in 1972.

★ ★ ★

Dirksen Senate Office Building

The second of the three Senate office buildings, the Everett M. Dirksen Senate Office Building covers a half-block area along Constitution Ave. directly east of the Russell building. The seven-story marble building houses Senators' office suites, committee offices and hearing rooms, and support services for the Senate. The building includes a 500-seat auditorium, a cafeteria, a buffet-style restaurant and a gift shop.

NEW S.O.B. *(above)*

The New Senate Office Building opened in 1955. In 1972 it was renamed for Sen. Everett M. Dirksen of Illinois.

PHOTO CREDIT:
Jim Berard

MOUNTAINS AND CLOUDS *(right)*

Alexander Calder's *Mountains and Clouds* graces the nine-story atrium of the Hart Senate Office Building.

PHOTO CREDIT:
Jeff Lesnik

The need for more space to supplement the Capitol and the original Senate office building became apparent to Senators in the 1930's and '40's, but it would take nearly 20 years to complete the project. The Architect of the Capitol was directed to draw up plans and cost estimates for a second Senate office building in 1941. The United States entered World War II later that year, so it wasn't until a few years after the war, in 1948-49, that a site for the new building was acquired and architects Otto R. Eggers and Daniel Paul Higgins were hired for the project. Still, ground-breaking did not take place until 1955 and Senators finally moved into their new building in 1958.

Originally called the New Senate Office Building, it was named for Sen. Everett McKinley Dirksen of Illinois in 1972.

★ ★ ★

THE HANDS OF TIME

When the Dirksen Building opened in 1958, it featured large, decorative clocks with solid brass hands.

It wasn't long before Senators noticed that the clocks did not keep good time. It turned out that the brass hands were too heavy for the clockworks to move and therefore the clocks continually ran slow.

The Architect of the Capitol solved the problem by installing cheaper, less attractive—but accurate—clocks in the building.

★ ★ ★

Hart Senate Office Building

In 1967, less than 10 years after the completion of the Dirksen building, the Senate was again feeling the pinch of a lack of office space. The Architect of the Capitol looked at enlarging the Dirksen building, but soon abandoned that concept and began plans for a third Senate office building.

The Hart Senate Office Building occupies the eastern half of the block on which the Dirksen building stands. That is, except for the southeast corner of the block, on which stands the Sewall-Belmont House. The historic building was the only private residence deliberately burned by the British in 1814 because it was used by American snipers to fire on the invaders as they marched to the Capitol. For more than a century, the house has served as a center of activity in the Women's Suffrage and Women's Rights movements. The architects who designed the Hart building were instructed to leave the Sewall-Belmont House alone.

Construction on the newest Senate office building began in 1975 and in 1982 Senators moved in.

The nine-story building provides over one million square feet of office space, including suites for

50 Senators. The office suites feature movable walls—"demountable partitions" in architectural terms—that allow each office to customize its floor plan.

The Hart building's construction was controversial from the start. Sen. William Proxmire of Wisconsin, a fiscal watchdog, called the building's plans "too palatial, too opulent," and gave one of his signature "Golden Fleece Awards" to his Senate colleagues for spending so much on the project. One critic called the design "Mussolini Modern."

Rampant inflation in the 1970's increased construction costs 187 percent. In 1978, the House, in an unusual move, killed a $54 million appropriation for completion of the building.

The Hart building even became an issue in the Senate elections of 1978, 1980 and 1982. Fiscal conservatives challenging incumbent Senators accused the Senate of building a "palace" for itself at taxpayers' expense. The criticism forced cutbacks in the building's amenities, including the elimination of a gymnasium and restaurant on the top floor.

The building became such a hot political topic by the time it was finished in 1982 that many senior Senators chose not to move into it. This created the unusual situation of the most junior Senators being forced to move into the newest, most modern office space on Capitol Hill. It also meant that some new Senators found their offices in the Hart building after winning election in part by criticizing the construction of the "palace."

★ ★ ★

MOUNTAINS, CLOUDS AND PAPER AIRPLANES

The Hart building's most striking feature is its central atrium, a T-shaped, light-filled, open space, nine stories high. The atrium is home to the black metal sculpture "Mountains and Clouds" by Alexander Calder. Installed in 1982,

the sculpture features a stationary piece (stabile) of triangular steel "mountains", weighing 39 tons (35.4 metric tons), on the floor of the atrium. A two-ton (1.8 metric-ton) hanging collection (mobile) of flat, black, aluminum "clouds" is suspended from the atrium's ceiling.

The large flat clouds provide a tempting target for pranksters who try to land paper airplanes on them from the upper floors of the atrium. It's not unusual to see several such aircraft resting atop the clouds, waiting for the mobile's next cleaning.

★ ★ ★

Cannon House Office Building

The Cannon House Office Building was built about the same time and by the same architectural firm as the Russell Senate Office Building. Completed in 1908, it was built in the beaux arts style like its sister across the Capitol lawn.

The original four-story building was home to 397 Member offices and 14 committee rooms. In 1913, a fifth floor was added. As additional House office buildings were constructed, the Cannon building has been remodeled to create fewer, but larger, office suites.

THE ORIGINAL H.O.B.

The Cannon House Office Building, shown here, and the Russell Senate Office Building are nearly mirror images of each other. Both buildings were designed in the beaux arts style. The Cannon building opened in 1908 and Russell opened a year later.

PHOTO CREDIT:
Jeff Lesnik

Originally called simply the House Office Building, in 1962 the building was named in honor of former Speaker of the House Joseph G. Cannon of Illinois.

★ ★ ★

"WHO DIED AND WHERE'S HIS OFFICE?"

Office suites on Capitol Hill are assigned according to seniority. When a suite becomes available because a Representative or Senator has left office, the most senior Members of the chamber are given the first crack at the vacant quarters. Less senior Members are then given the chance to move into the office vacated by the Members with more seniority.

This typically happens after an election, but, until recently, such moves could take place whenever an office suite became available, including when a Member died in office. The death of a Member of Congress is traditionally marked by lowering the flags on the Capitol and the Congressional office buildings to half-staff. One long-time office manager for a Representative said that whenever she drove to work and saw the flags at half-staff, the first thing she would do was call the Superintendent's office and ask, "Who died and where's his office?"

In the House, these mid-term moves could become very costly and disruptive. Just one vacancy could trigger several moves as junior Members tried to move up to larger or more convenient offices. So, in 1992, the House changed its rules to restrict office moves to once every two years, the time immediately following the Congressional election.

Thanks to this new rule, a newly elected Member who comes into office during the Congressional term moves into the office vacated by his or her predecessor. So, the most junior Member can occupy a highly desirable office suite, at least until the end of the term.

★ ★ ★

The Longworth House Office Building

Despite expansion, overcrowding in the original (Cannon) House Office Building by 1925 led the House to begin planning for a second office building.

The new building, named in 1962 for former Speaker Nicholas Longworth of Ohio, was built just west of the Cannon building and was completed in 1933. Built in the neoclassical revival style, it was designed by the local firm Allied Architects of Washington, Inc.

At 600,000 square feet, it is the smallest of the three main House office buildings. Along with Member suites and committee rooms, the Longworth building also contains a food court, credit union branch, gift shop, and post office.

GUCCI GULCH

Room 1101 of the Longworth House Office Building is the hearing room for the House Ways and Means Committee. With a seating capacity of 450, it is the largest of the House committee hearing rooms. The full House met in this room in 1949 and 1950 while the House Chamber in the Capitol was being remodeled.

The Ways and Means Committee has jurisdiction over tax policy. Taxes, and the right tax loopholes, can greatly affect a company's profits. So, businesses and industry groups hire expensive lobbyists to monitor the committee's activities and try to influence it to vote for policies most favorable to their clients.

The lobbyists who attend the Ways and Means Committee hearings are known for their expensive clothing. So much so that the hallway outside the hearing room is known as "Gucci Gulch" for the designer shoes they wear.

★ ★ ★

Rayburn House Office Building

The newest and largest of the principal House office buildings is the Rayburn building, completed in 1965. It is located along Independence Avenue west of the Cannon and Longworth buildings.

The building houses 169 Member office suites, each with three rooms, a reception area, kitchen, a Member's bathroom and a staff bathroom, although the kitchens and staff bathrooms in many of the suites have been sacrificed for more storage or equipment space. Nine committees are also based in the Rayburn building. It has four main floors, plus a basement, sub-basement and three parking levels.

The building's amenities include a cafeteria, deli, banquet rooms, a first aid station, fully equipped radio and television taping facilities, a Library of Congress research room, post office, credit union branch and a Members' gymnasium.

At the time the Rayburn building was under construction, the Cannon building was still known simply as the House Office Building, and the Longworth building was officially known as the New House Office Building. As local commentators speculated on the name for the building under construction, one suggested calling it the Really New House Office Building. Instead, the House decided to name it in honor of Sam Rayburn of Texas, who was Speaker of the House when the building was authorized. The other House Office Buildings were also dedicated to the Speakers who held the office when each of the buildings was authorized.

★ ★ ★

PARDON MY BACK

The stern visage of Sam Rayburn stares out from an oil painting by artist Tom Lea and greets visitors to the building bearing his name as they enter the South Capitol Street door. The former Speaker's glower is still more flattering than the view of the former Speaker that used to welcome visitors at the building's other main entrance.

Shortly after the Rayburn building was opened, the Texas State Society of Washington donated a life-size bronze statue of the late Speaker by Felix de Weldon. The sculpture was placed in a light-filled foyer at the base of two marble staircases. When it was first installed, the work was positioned so that Rayburn faced toward a wall of windows and glass doors that opened into the building's central courtyard.

The problem with the statue's placement, though, was that people coming into the building from Independence Avenue, across the hall from the statue, were greeted by the sight of Rayburn's coattails.

The matter was solved a short time later when the statue was turned around to face the entrance instead of the courtyard.

★ ★ ★

FACING FORWARD

A life-size statue of Sam Rayburn greets visitors to the House Office Building that bears his name. When it was first installed, the statue faced the building's courtyard, giving an unflattering view of the former Speaker to folks coming into the building. It was soon turned around to face the entrance.

PHOTO CREDIT:
Jeff Lesnik

The House Annexes

Besides the three main House office buildings, House offices occupy another building near the Capitol. Originally known as House Annex II, it was renamed in 1990 after former House Minority Leader and President, Gerald R. Ford of Michigan. The Ford House Office Building at Second and D Streets SW, once housed the FBI fingerprint lab. It is now home to the House computer center as well as additional services and staff offices. No Members' offices are located in the building.

Who Are These Guys?

Here's a little background on the men who have lent their names to the Congressional office buildings:

Joseph G. Cannon, Illinois

A Republican from Illinois, "Uncle Joe" Cannon is known for his iron grip on power in the House during his four terms as Speaker (1903-1911). During his Speakership, Cannon also held the powerful post of Chairman of the Rules Committee and wielded virtually total control over the activities of the House.

Cannon lost the Speakership when the Democrats gained the House majority in 1911, and he was defeated for reelection to his Congressional seat in 1912. Two years later, Cannon returned to Congress for four more terms, retiring in 1923. Cannon's total control of the House led to new rules to prevent future Speakers from wielding such unchallenged authority.

Everett McKinley Dirksen, Illinois

After eight terms in the House, Republican Everett Dirksen was elected to the Senate in 1950. Dirksen served three terms in the Senate, and was Minority Leader from 1959 to 1969. A leading conservative, Dirksen opposed most of President Franklin Roosevelt's New Deal programs in the 1930's and '40's. He continued to champion conservative causes during his Senate career. However, Dirksen broke with fellow conservatives on several crucial issues of the 1960's, supporting such progressive measures as the Civil Rights Act, the Voting Rights Act and the Nuclear Test Ban Treaty.

Dirksen spoke with a deep, distinctive, resonant voice. In 1966, he narrated the recording *Gallant Men*, which won a Grammy award for Best Spoken Word, Drama or Documentary Recording the following year.

Gerald R. Ford, Michigan

Gerald Ford is the only President to achieve the office without having first been elected President or Vice President. As a Republican Representative from Michigan, Ford served in Congress from 1949 to 1973 and held the post of Minority Leader for nearly 10 years. In 1973, during the height of the Watergate scandal, President Richard Nixon needed a new Vice President following the resignation of Spiro Agnew. The beleaguered President knew he had to choose someone of unquestionable integrity. He chose Ford.

When Nixon himself resigned the following year, Ford assumed the Presidency. Shortly after taking office, Ford made the bold and controversial step of issuing a Presidential pardon to Nixon. That decision may have ended his political career. Ford was defeated for a full term in 1976 by Jimmy Carter.

The Ford House Office Building is the only one of the four House office buildings not named for a former Speaker of the House.

Philip A. Hart, Michigan

A veteran of World War II, wounded at Normandy, Sen. Philip A. Hart served from 1958 to 1976. The Michigan Democrat became known as the "conscience of the Senate" for his principled stands on the issues of the day.

Nicholas Longworth, Ohio

Nicholas Longworth served as Speaker of the House in the 69th through 71st Congresses, 1925-1931. During his term as Speaker, the House began construction on its second office building. First called the New House Office Building, it was completed in 1933, two years after Longworth's death. The building was renamed the Longworth House Office Building in 1962. An inscription in the marbled foyer of the building reads, in part, "A constructive leader, his judgment, vigor and humanity will remain unsurpassed in the annals of American leadership.".

Sam Rayburn, Texas

The longest-serving Speaker of the House in Congressional history, Sam Rayburn held the post for a total of 19 years. First elected to the House in 1913, Rayburn served 48 years until his death in 1961. Rayburn was elected Speaker in 1940 following the death of William B. Bankhead. He was re-elected Speaker in nine of the next 10 Congressional terms, the only interruption coming when the Republicans controlled the House in 1955-56.

Richard Brevard Russell , Georgia

A former Governor of Georgia, Democrat Richard Russell came to the U.S. Senate in 1933 and served for 38 years. During his tenure, Russell chaired a number of powerful committees, including the Armed Services Committee, then later the Appropriations Committee. Russell also served as President Pro Tempore of the Senate (the official presiding officer in the absence of the Vice President) during his final years in office.

BY THE NUMBERS

Visitors to the House office buildings are often confused by the room numbering system.

Each room or suite has a unique address. In the Cannon building, they carry three-digit numbers and the first digit signifies the floor. So, Room 345 is on the third floor of the Cannon building.

In the Longworth building, all room numbers carry a four-digit number and begin with a 1. The first digit identifies the number as a Longworth address, and the second digit signifies the floor. Room 1723 can be found on the seventh floor of Longworth.

Likewise, all Rayburn addresses carry a four-digit number beginning with the number 2. Like Longworth offices, the second digit identifies the floor. So, Room 2167 is on the Rayburn building's first floor.

At least one Member of Congress thought the House numbering system is so confusing that it should be changed. Rep. Marcy Kaptur of Ohio broached the subject with Architect of the Capitol Alan Hantman at an Appropriations Committee hearing in 2002.

"Have you done a survey of lost tourists?" Kaptur asked the Architect. Kaptur suggested renumbering the rooms, but the Architect suggested improving signs and installing information kiosks on the Capitol grounds would help relieve the confusion.

The Senate office buildings use a variation of the room numbers used in the Capitol, where all rooms on the Senate side of the building begin with the letter "S." The Senate uses the prefixes SR, SD and SH to indicate whether an address can be found in the Russell, Dirksen or Hart Senate Office Building, and a three digit number with the first digit identifying the floor. SH-719 is on the seventh floor of Hart.

14

THE CAPITOL UNDERGROUND

The U.S. Capitol complex contains a maze of underground passageways connecting the Capitol with the House and Senate office buildings and the Library of Congress. Using these tunnels, a person can travel from the Hart building on the Senate side in a U-shaped route to the Adams building of the Library of Congress without once stepping outside. (The underground route would cover 2.5 miles (3.75 kilometers) and take the walker through five other buildings, including the Capitol. A much more direct—and practical—surface route would cover a distance of only three blocks.)

"Chariots of Democracy"

These passages date back to the early 20th century, when the House and Senate built their first office buildings separate from the Capitol. The new House building, now called the Cannon House Office Building, was connected to the Capitol by an underground walkway.

The Senate went one better and employed electric automobiles, made by Studebaker, to shuttle Senators through a tunnel from the Senate Office Building (now the Russell building) to the Capitol and back.

The Senate later replaced the Studebakers with an electric trolley with open cars and wicker seats. Dubbed the "Toonerville Trolley" by Senators, the subway began operation in 1911. One of the old subway cars is on display in the lower rotunda of the Russell building.

In 1959, the Senate replaced the old trolleys with a totally new system, and extended the trains to its other office building, now known as the Dirksen building. The $6 million project constructed a pair of tracks from a station beneath the Senate steps of the Capitol to each of the two office buildings. The old trolleys were replaced with

sleek, modern, partially enclosed, 18-passenger cars. When the new subway was dedicated, the Senate chaplain called the new cars "chariots of democracy."

The ceremony culminated in a spontaneous race from the Dirksen building to the Capitol, with Sen. Dennis Chavez of New Mexico and Architect of the Capitol J. George Stewart in one car and Sen. Jennings Randolph of West Virginia and several reporters in the other.

Others were not so impressed with the new subway system. The modern cars lacked some of the nostalgic appeal of the old wicker cars. Their steel wheels made for a noisy, bumpy ride. Sen. William Fulbright of Arkansas called the new cars "incredibly vulgar, poorly designed, combining all the bad taste of the Western world." He complained about "all that chrome" (which was actually stainless steel), the "cheap upholstery" and the "loud, clattering ride." Fulbright said the old Toonerville Trolleys were smoother, quieter and had "a certain quality or charm about them."

Fulbright suggested taking out the new subway cars and replacing them with rubber-tired Jeeps.

Two years after the new cars began service, the Architect of the Capitol responded to Senators' complaints and refitted the cars with hard rubber tires for a smoother, quieter ride.

(When the Dirksen building opened in 1958, a fleet of three automobiles shuttled Senators to the Capitol and back on surface streets until the subway was extended to the new building.)

While Senators rode to the Capitol, Representatives walked. The House had only a walkway connecting its office buildings to the Capitol until the Rayburn House Office Building was opened in 1965. The building is linked to the Capitol by a 630-foot (189-meter) two-track subway, with two 24-passenger, manually operated cars similar to the ones serving the Senate buildings.

(opposite page)

A LONESOME WALK

Congressman and future President Gerald R. Ford walks alone through the tunnel connecting the Capitol with the Cannon House Office Building.

PHOTO CREDIT:
Gerald Ford Presidential Library,
Neg. no. H0012-1

GETTING AROUND UNDER GROUND, THEN AND NOW

When the first House and Senate office buildings were completed a century ago, tunnels were built to connect the new buildings with the Capitol. Senators employed electric cars (top) to ferry them back and forth. In 1994, the Senate put into service a new, fully automated system with enclosed cars.

PHOTO CREDIT:
(top)
Library of Congress.
Neg. no. LC-USA7-12566
(bottom)
Jeff Lesnik

Bullet Trains

In 1995, the Senate subway went through yet another transformation. A new fully automated system replaced the 1959 cars on the route serving the Dirksen building, which had been extended to the new Hart building in 1982. The new system consists of four three-car trains making a continuous loop from the Capitol to the Hart building, with stops at the Dirksen building each way. The new cars are fully enclosed. (A common complaint about the old open-top cars was that the wind messed up Senators' hair. No such problem with the new system.)

The red-white and-blue fiberglass cars resemble bullet trains and are run by computer from a central control room at the Dirksen stop. However, even this state-of-the-art transportation system was not without its bugs.

When the new trains first began running, they were prone to frequent breakdowns. Because the cars were fully enclosed and the doors opened and closed automatically, many Senators found themselves trapped on the subway on the way to votes or important meetings. The automatic doors were a major source of the problems.

The old manual system had a human operator on each car. The driver could watch for Senators wanting to board and delay departure, if necessary. The new automated system has no operator on board, and, when it first began service, Senators would often hold the doors open for approaching colleagues. The computer would interpret this as a malfunction and shut down the system, stopping all trains wherever they may be in their route. Senators soon learned not to hold the doors open.

The new Senate subway is very democratic. It treats everyone equally and waits for no one.

VOTE THIS WAY, CONGRESSMAN.

At the terminal where the House subway arrives in the Capitol, a pair of escalators leads to and from an elevator bank one flight up. The elevators then take passengers into the Capitol itself and provides Members with the quickest route to the House chamber. A sign at the base of the escalators directs users to stay to the right.

Before 1995, when the Democrats controlled the House, the sign read, "Keep Left."

The sign's message was more practical than political. The elevators at the next level are to the left of the escalators. By having the left escalator carry people up to that level, Members on their way to the House floor could make a quick left turn into the first elevator without having to cross a line of people waiting to board the down escalator. This saved precious steps—and seconds—for legislators late for a recorded vote.

When the Republicans took control of the House majority in 1995, they were apparently uncomfortable with Members encountering a sign instructing them to "keep left" while on the way to vote. They had the escalators reversed and changed the sign to "Keep Right."

POLITICAL DIRECTIONS

These escalators take Members from the Capitol terminal of the House subway to elevators to the House Chamber. Originally, the left escalator traveled up, the right escalator came down, and the sign read "Keep Left." When the Republicans took control of the House in 1995, they reversed the escalators and changed the sign.

PHOTO CREDIT:
Jeff Lesnik

15

THE NATION'S CAPITAL: WASHINGTON, D.C.

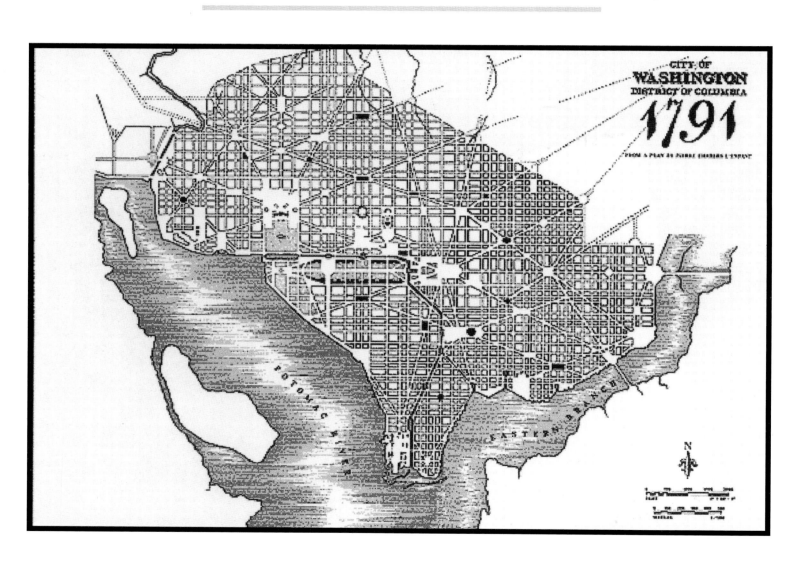

When the Constitutional Convention met in Philadelphia in 1787 to create a new government for the United States, the Founders determined that the government should be located in a federal district over which Congress had sole control. They just didn't know where that district would be located.

During the Revolutionary War and in the early days of the nation's independence, Congress had no permanent home. Cities such as Philadelphia and York, Pennsylvania; Trenton, New Jersey; Annapolis, Maryland; and New York City served as the nation's capital from time to time. In 1791, President George Washington selected a 100-square-mile diamond of land straddling the Potomac River for the new federal district. About 70 percent of the territory was carved from Maryland and the rest from Virginia. The territory was ceded by the two states and private landowners were compensated for their property. The new federal enclave was named the District of Columbia and the capital city established there was named Washington.

The district also incorporated two existing cities. Alexandria, Virginia, and Georgetown, Maryland, which became Alexandria, D.C., and Georgetown, D.C.

In 1846, Congress returned the portion of the district south of the river to Virginia. This included the city of Alexandria and what is now Arlington County. The area now includes the Pentagon, Reagan National Airport, Arlington National Cemetery, and a population of more than 300,000.

Across the river, the city of Washington grew steadily. What began as a cluster of government buildings between Capitol Hill and Foggy Bottom soon encroached on neighboring Georgetown. In 1871, Washington absorbed its neighbor, and Georgetown, D.C., ceased to exist as a separate city. Modern day Washington encompasses the entire territory of the District of Columbia, and the distinction that once existed between these two entities has disappeared.

Although Congress has ultimate authority over the affairs of the District, it does permit a degree of local control. The D.C. government functions in many ways like a state government, regulating businesses, enforcing the criminal and civil laws, and issuing drivers licenses and automobile registrations. It also functions as a municipal government, responsible for such things as street maintenance, garbage collection, and local schools.

The D.C. government is run by an elected mayor and city council.

TAXATION WITHOUT REPRESENTATION

The District of Columbia is a unique political entity. It is a federal district over which Congress has the ultimate authority.

The D.C. government provides services comparable to those provided by state governments, but the District is not a state. Since the Constitution limits membership in Congress to representatives of the states, the people who live in the Nation's Capital have no voting representation in Congress. They do have a delegate to the House of Representatives who can vote only in committee, but there is no representation at all in the Senate. In this way, the people who live within sight of the Capitol dome are given the same status as those who live in offshore territories, such as Puerto Rico, Guam and American Samoa, with one major difference: residents of the territories pay no federal income tax, but residents of the District of Columbia do.

When the original 13 colonies rebelled against British rule, they were protesting the imposition of taxes by a Parliament in which they had no voice. "Taxation without representation is tyranny," was their cry.

In 2000, Washington, D.C., Mayor Anthony Williams raised the same cry on behalf of his city by imprinting "Taxation without Representation" on the District's license plates.

Before he left the White House, President Bill Clinton ordered license plates with the new slogan to be displayed on the Presidential limousine.

Upon taking office, Clinton's successor, George W. Bush, ordered the plates removed and replaced with plates bearing the old slogan, "Celebrate and Discover."

★ ★ ★

The Geometry of the Geography

When Pierre Charles L'Enfant laid out the streets of Washington, he designed the city in a geometric grid pattern and divided it into four sections or quadrants: Northeast, Northwest, Southeast and Southwest.

L'Enfant centered the street system on the Capitol, so all street numbers begin there and the numbers rise as you travel away from the Capitol. North Capitol St. and South Capitol St. divide the quadrants east and west. East Capitol St. and the National Mall divide the quadrants north and south. It is important to note the quadrant for any address, since there could be an identical number and street in each of the four quadrants. The quadrants are not identical in size. Northwest is the largest of the four; Southwest is the smallest.

Numbered streets run north and south, and lettered streets run east and west. L'Enfant skipped the letter J, and X, Y and Z were never used. Some addresses on I St. list it as "Eye St." so as not to be confused with 1—or First— St. In the sections of the city beyond W St., the east-west streets are named alphabetically.

A St. NE and NW were eliminated near the Capitol when the new north and south wings were added and the grounds expanded during the 1800's. West of the Capitol, where the National Mall runs past the Smithsonian museums, the streets have been renamed Jefferson Drive and Madison Drive. B St. NE and NW are now called Constitution Ave. B St. SE and SW are now Independence Ave.

Avenues named for states emanate like spokes from circles and squares throughout the city. The most famous is Pennsylvania Avenue, which connects the Capitol with the White House.

WASHINGTON'S CANALS

This photo from 1858 shows one of the canals that used to run along the National Mall. At right center is the U.S. Botanic Garden's first conservatory, and the Capitol's new iron dome rises in the background.

PHOTO CREDIT:
Library of Congress.
Neg. no. LC-USZ62-80394

★ ★ ★

DON'T CALL IT A SWAMP

Washington, D.C. was built in a swamp —Not!

Many stories about Washington's early years perpetuate the myth that the city was built on a swamp. This makes local historians bristle. "George Washington would never have selected a swamp for his new capital,"they rightfully argue.

The city's reputation as a swamp thing dates back to the early 19th Century. European diplomats, accustomed to the more refined surroundings of Paris, Rome and Vienna found Washington to be primitive by comparison. Construction throughout the the young city created a great deal of mud. Canals filled with sewage and garbage gave off pungent fumes,and the city's infamous humid summers gave critics even more ammunition.

In truth, the city was built on land that had been mostly farms and forest, and marshy wetlands lined the banks of the Potomac. While not yet a cosmopolitan city to rival the European capitals, Washington was hardly a swamp.

Today, Washington's streets are paved, the canals, have been covered, the Lincoln and Jefferson memorials stand on landfills where there were once marshes, and modern air conditioning has mitigated the summer humidity. It is now a city of monuments and open spaces. When the cherry blossoms bloom each Spring, Washington is the most beautiful capital city in the world.

Take that, Paris!

★ ★ ★

A Capitol Chronology

1790	Passage of the Residence Act sets in motion the federal government's move from New York to Philadelphia and, finally, Washington, D.C.
1793	Architect William Thornton wins $500 and a building lot for his design of the Capitol. President Washington lays the first cornerstone.
1800	Work is completed on the north (Senate) wing. The Senate, House, Supreme Court and Library of Congress move in. Congress meets for the first time in the Capitol.
1807	The House moves into the completed south wing.
1808-09	Latrobe rebuilds the north wing, creating new chambers for the Senate and Supreme Court
1814	British invaders during the War of 1812 set fire to the Capitol, leaving a "magnificent ruin."
1815	Congress takes up temporary residence in the Old Brick Capitol.
1819	Congress returns to the Capitol following post-fire renovations.
1829	The Capitol is completed with addition of the center Rotunda and wooden dome.
1826	A fire in the Library of Congress prompts removal of firewood and other flammables to storage areas in new terraces to be built along the West Front.
1832	Running water is installed in the Capitol.
1840's	Gas lighting is installed.
1851	Construction begins on the new House and Senate wing.
1851	Fire guts the Library of Congress. A new, fireproof cast-iron room is designed.
1857-59	The House and Senate move into their new quarters.
1861-65	The Capitol is used as a hospital, bakery and barracks during the Civil War.
1863	The new cast-iron dome is completed and topped with the Statue of Freedom.
1865	Brumidi fresco *Apotheosis of Washington* is completed.
1868	Work completed on new House and Senate wings.
1874	First elevator is installed.
1884-1891	Capitol grounds are improved; new marble terraces along the West Front are built.

1890-1900	Electric lighting and modern plumbing are installed.
1897	The Library of Congress moves to new quarters (now called the Jefferson Building).
1898	A gas explosion rocks the Senate wing.
1901	Roof areas of the original Capitol building are fireproofed.
1908	First House Office Building (Cannon) is completed.
1909	First Senate Office Building (Russell) is completed.
1933	New (Longworth) House Office Building is opened.
1935	The Supreme Court moves into its own building after 135 years in the Capitol.
1949-50	The House and Senate Chambers are remodeled; roofs are rebuilt.
1958	New (Dirksen) Senate Office Building is opened.
1958-62	The East Front is extended. The old sandstone facade is copied in marble.
1965	Rayburn House Office Building is occupied.
1982	Hart Senate Office Building is occupied.
1987	Work is completed on the restoration of the West Front.
1993	West Front courtyards are filled in with offices and meeting rooms.
1993	The Statue of Freedom is removed from the dome, refurbished and reinstalled.
2001	New anti-terrorism measures are installed.
2005	Projected completion date for the new underground Visitors Center.

THE CONGRESSIONAL SMITHY

The Capitol blacksmith shop. circa 1908.

PHOTO CREDIT:
Library of Congress
Neg. no. LC-USZ62-51473

Sources and Bibliography

Sources

Associated Press

Baltimore Sun

B&O Railroad Museum, Baltimore

Capitol Hostesses, Richmond, Va.

City Paper

Congress Daily

Congressional Directory

Congressional Record

Detroit News

Everett McKinley Dirksen Congressional
    Leadership Center, Pekin, Illinois

Georgetown Heritage Trust

The Hill

Historical Society of Washington

Library of Congress

Life

Look

National Archives and Records Administration

National Enquirer

National Geographic

National Park Service

New York Times

Office of the Architect of the Capitol

Office of the Clerk of the House

Office of the Curator of the Capitol

Office of the Senate Curator

Office of the Senate Historian

Parade

Robert A. Taft Memorial Carillon Dedication Program

Roll Call

U.S. Capitol Guide Service

U.S. Capitol Historical Society

U.S. Senate Library

Washington Daily News

Washington Herald

Washington Post

Washington Star

Washington Times

Washingtoniana Division, D.C. Public Library

WETA Magazine

World Almanac and Book of Facts, 2002

Bibliography

Aikman, Lonelle. We the People: The Story of the United States Capitol. Washington: U.S. Capitol Historical Society, 1991.

Alexander, John. Ghosts—Washington's Most Famous Ghost Stories. Arlington: Washington Book Trading Company, 1988.

Allen, William C. History of the United States Capitol. Washington: U.S. Government Printing Office, 2001.

Atwater, Maxine H. Capital Tales: True stories about Washington's heroes, villains & belles. Bethesda: Mercury Press, 1996.

Boller, Paul F., Jr. Congressional Anecdotes. New York: Oxford University Press, 1991.

Byrd, Robert C. The Senate 1789-1989. 4 vols. Washington: U.S. Government Printing Office, 1993.

Carpenter, Frank G., Frances Carpenter, ed. Carp's Washington. New York: McGraw Hill, 1960.

Clemens, Samuel Langhorne, Edgar M. Branch, ed. Mark Twain's Letters to the Muscatine Journal. Chicago: Mark Twain Association of America, 1942.

Cline, Patricia Edwards. Strange and Supernatural Animals. New York: Dodd, Mead & Co., 1979.

Eigen, Lewis D., and **Jonathan P. Siegel.** The Macmillan Dictionary of Political Quotations. New York: Macmillan Publishing Company, 1993.

Evelyn, Douglas E., and **Paul Dickson.** On This Spot. Washington: National Geographic Society, 1992, 1999

Forman, Stephen M. Political Humor in America. Carlisle, Mass.: Discovery Enterprises, 1998.

Hays, Brooks. A Hotbed of Tranquility. New York: The McMillan Company, 1968.

Huston, James H. To Make All Laws. Washington: U.S. Government Printing Office, 1989.

Kennedy, John F. Profiles in Courage (Memorial Edition). New York: Harper & Row, 1964.

Lamb, Brian. C-SPAN: America's Town Hall. Washington: Acropolis Books Ltd., 1988.

Lynam, Marshall L. Stories I Never Told the Speaker. Dallas: Three Forks Press, 1998.

McCarthy, Eugene J. An American Bestiary. Red Wing: Lone Oak Press, 2000.

McRae, Sherwin. The Houdon Statue, Its History and Value. Richmond: Superintendent of Public Printing, 1873.

Prime, Samuel Irenæus. The Life of Samuel F. B. Morse. New York: D. Appleton, 1875.

United States. Architect of the Capitol. *Art in the United States Capitol.* Washington: U.S. Government Printing Office, 1976.

Washington, George. *Last Will and Testament.* Washington: A. Jackson, 1868.

Wolanin, Barbara A. Constantino Brumidi, *Artist of the Capitol.* Washington: U.S. Government Printing Office, 1998

Internet Sources

Architect of the Capitol (www.aoc.gov)

Center for American Women in Politics, Rutgers University (www.cawp.rutgers.edu)

JunkScience.com (www.junkscience.com)

Library of Congress (www.loc.gov)

National Archives (www.nara.gov)

National Park Service (www.nps.gov)

Pensacola Archaeology Lab
(http://sites.gulf.net/pal/)

The Political Graveyard
(www.politicalgraveyard.com)

U.S. Capitol Historical Society (www.uschs.org)

U.S. House of Representatives (www.house.gov)

U.S. Senate (www.senate.gov)

PAGES AT PLAY *(top right)*

Senate pages take advantage of a fresh snowfall to engage in a snowball fight on the Capitol grounds in this photo from the 1920's.

CAPITOL CHIEFS *(bottom right)*

Native American chiefs Frank Seelatse and Jimmy Noah Saluskin of the Yakama tribe pose in front of the Capitol during a visit to Washington in 1927.

Helpful Information

The U.S. Capitol is located at the west end of the National Mall in Washington, D.C. It is easy to get to by public transportation, but public parking near the Capitol is scarce. On the Washington Metro (subway) system, the Capitol South station on the Orange and Blue lines and the Union Station stop on the Red line are the most convenient for visitors to the Capitol. Union Station is also served by Amtrak and two local commuter rail lines, and is also the hub for many bus tours of the city.

For passes to watch Congress in action from the House and Senate Visitors Galleries, and for other visitor information about the Capitol and Washington, D.C., contact your Senators or Representative. (See below.) They can also help you arrange for tours of the Capitol, White House and F.B.I. (when available).

You can also get information about public tours of the Capitol by calling the Capitol Guide Service at 202-225-6827.

For additional information about visiting the Capitol, check out the Architect of the Capitol's website, www.aoc.gov.

Online information about other Washington attractions and amenities can be had from the National Park Service at www.nps.gov, the Smithsonian Institution at www.si.edu, and the Washington Convention and Tourism Corporation, at www.washington.org.

Who's My Congressman?

If you don't know the name or phone number of your elected representatives in Congress, there are several ways to find out.

Senators and Representatives have offices in their home states. There may be one in your town. Check the telephone book under U.S. Government.

If not, your local library or courthouse should have this information on file.

The Capitol operator at (202)224-3121 can direct your call to your Representative or Senator's Washington office.

On the Internet, the Senate website, www.senate.gov, has listings of Senators by state. The House website, www.house.gov, has a feature that allows you to find your Representative by entering your ZIP code. It also lists Representatives by state.

About the Author
Jim Berard

A Capitol Hill press secretary since 1987, Jim Berard spends much of his spare time helping visitors to Washington learn about and appreciate our national landmarks. He serves as a volunteer for Meridian International Center in Washington, providing tours of the Capitol for visiting foreign dignitaries. He is also a volunteer for the National Park Service, providing tours and visitor information at his other favorite Washington monument, the Washington Monument.

Born in Joliet, Illinois, Jim is a graduate of Joliet Catholic High School and Northern Illinois University. He has also done graduate work at the University of Iowa.

Jim's first book, *The Flying Cat and Other Amazing Stories of the Washington Monument*, was published by EPM Publications in 2000. It has been the subject of articles in the Associated Press, *The Washington Times*, the Capitol Hill newspapers *Roll Call* and *The Hill*, and other publications. Jim has also appeared on the Discovery Channel and the History Channel as well as Washington's local MHz Network, cable News Channel 8 and WMAL radio.

Jim's real job is with the House Committee on Transportation and Infrastructure, where he serves as Communications Director for the Democratic leadership of the committee. He has held similar positions in the personal offices of Sen. Kent Conrad of North Dakota and Rep. James L. Oberstar of Minnesota.

PHOTO CREDIT: Jeff Lesnik

Before coming to Washington, Jim spent 15 years as a radio journalist at stations in Illinois, Iowa and Minnesota. From 1982 to 1987, he produced *Common Ground*, a nationally distributed radio documentary series on world affairs, for the Stanley Foundation of Muscatine, Iowa. Prior to that he won several awards for news and editorials as News and Public Affairs Director at radio station KWEB-KRCH in Rochester, Minnesota.

Jim is a member of the U.S. Capitol Historical Society and the Historical Society of Washington.